MACHINIST SECOND YEAR MCQ

OBJECTIVE QUESTION ANSWERS

MANOJ DOLE

Made with ♥ on the Notion Press Platform
www.notionpress.com

Digitization is the need of the time. In the future, training in industrial training institutes will need to be conducted using online internet to make training more convenient and easy. E-books containing a set of MCQ questions will be made available to the trainees as they need to be more accustomed to the multiple choice questions MCQ to prepare for the online exams taking place in their industrial training institutes.

With all these factors in mind, Mr. Manoj Madhukar Dole Instructor, Industrial Training Institute, Satara, has written books according to the new annual system and NSQF-5 syllabus. And they've created theoretical mobile apps and blogs to make training easier, and made all these educational materials available for download on the world famous websites Google Play Store, Amazon and Apple Book Store.

The books were published by Hon'ble Joint Director Shri Rajendra Ghume Saheb Regional Office of Vocational Education and Training, Pune on 9/1/2019, at this time Shri Prakash Saigavkar Saheb Principal Government Industrial Training Institute Aundh Pune, Shri Tukaram Misal Saheb Principal Govt. Q. Sanstha Satara, Shri Sachin Dhumal Saheb District Vocational Education and Training Officer Satara, Shri Yatin Pargaonkar Saheb Principal Govt. Q. Sanstha Kolhapur, Shri Vikas Teke Saheb Inspector Vocational Education and Training Regional Office Pune, Palekar Foods Products Pvt. Ltd. Entrepreneurial Chairman of Satara Mr. Nilkanthrao Palekar Saheb, Chairman of Hira Foods Mr. Ibrahim Baba Tamboli Saheb, Mrs. Shalmali Pawar Headmaster Government Technical School Center Satara and other dignitaries were present on the occasion.

Contents

Prologue

Machinist Second Year MCQ is a simple Book for ITI Engineering Course Lift and Escalator Mechanic, Second Year, Sem- 3 & 4, Revised NSQ F-5 Syllabus in 2022, It contains objective questions with underlined & bold correct answers MCQ covering all topics including all about the latest & Important about cutting tools, milling operation like boring, gear cutting, spline, Basic electrical equipment and sensors, CNC turning operation, CNC milling operation, operation and part programming, simple repair and maintenance work, machining of some complicated components like bevel gears, plate components, worm wheel, worm thread, and lots more.

We add new question answers with each new version. Please email us in case of any errors/omissions. This is arguably the largest and best e-Book for All engineering multiple choice questions and answers.

As a student you can use it for your exam prep. This Book is also useful for professors to refresh material.

Foreword

Vocational education and training is imparted through the Department of Vocational Education and Training through the Department of Business Education and Business Practical to supply multi-skilled artisans in line with the rapidly growing demand in the industrial sector in the 21st century. All the occupations within the institutions are important, as the trainees from these occupations develop multi-skills as per the demands of the industry.

with the noble intention of making available MCQ e-books suitable for all businesses, considering that all the examinations in all the industries in the industrial sector are conducted online and include MCQ method questions. Mr. Manoj Madhukar Dole has written a very good e-book on MCQ method as per the new annual syllabus. This e-book will definitely be a guide for all the trainees, trainee candidates, training instructors and others concerned.

The author of the book is Mr. Manoj Madhukar Dole, Instructor Gov. ITI Satara has 17 years of training experience. Written as a new annual pattern, this e-book incorporates modern digital QR Code technology to understand the layout, simple language, and simple syntax, diagrams and videos for each subject. So I am sure that this e-book will definitely be useful for in-depth study and exam practice. The work they have done is certainly commendable.

Mr. Tukaram Misal
Principal Government Industrial Training Institute Satara.

Preface

DGET New Delhi and CSTARI Kolkata have been implementing an annual pattern for all businesses in ITI since the August 2018 session. The examination system will also be changed and it will be online from this year and since all the questions are of Objective Type (MCQ), the trainees are in dire need of in-depth study. It is with this in mind that we are delighted to present the books based on the old NIMI pattern and a complete overview of the new annual pattern, and we hope that these books will be a guide for all business directors and trainees. Is.

For writing these books, Johar Awate Saheb, Principal of ITI Akluj. Former Principal of ITI Satara Saigavkar Saheb, Assistant Director Shri Chandrakant Dhekne Saheb Regional Office of Vocational Education and Training, Pune, District Vocational Education and Training Officer Sachin Dhumal Saheb and Headmaster Government Technical School Kendra Shalmali Pawar Madam and son Adhiraj Dole, mother Kusum Dole, I am very grateful to my father Madhukar Dole and wife Ashwini Dole for their special guidance and cooperation from time to time.

Also, in a very short period of time, the book was reviewed by Shri Rajendra Ghume Saheb, Joint Director, Vocational Education and Training Regional Office, Pune, for his invaluable time in publishing the book. I am sincerely grateful for their feedback.

I am grateful to the Instructor of ITI Satara for there continuous support from the very beginning of writing the book.

From this book, I consider myself blessed to have shared my thoughts on e-learning with you. I will not claim that this book is perfect, because considering the perfection, this book is an attempt and is in its infancy. They will be valuable for improvement if they are tested and suggested.

Manoj Dole
Dated 9/1/2019

Acknowledgements

The industrial training and theoretical examination system of our industrial training institutes and these changes have been accepted by the craft instructors and the trainees. Theoretical examinations conducted in your industrial training institutes are also conducted online. Since these examinations are of multiple choice MCQ method, the trainees will need to get more practice of such questions.

With all these considerations in mind, Mr. Manoj Madhukar, Director, Dole Crafts, Katari Industrial Training Institute, Satara, has done a thorough study and with his diligent work and added his keen intellect, according to the new annual system and NSQF-5 syllabus, e-book of Katari and other machine trades. -Book) and they have created mobile apps and blogs on theoretical topics to make training easier and have made all these educational materials available for download on the world famous websites Google Play Store, Amazon and Apple Book Store. Training has been made easier by creating a print version and using advanced techniques like QR Code.

All these educational materials will definitely be a guide for all the trainees for in-depth study and for the craft instructors and other concerned who are imparting vocational training.

CHAPTER ONE

Machinist Second Year MCQ Drawings

Online Test Exam

ITI Books

CNC Course

AutoCAD CAM

JOB & Apprentice

Online Theory

Computer Course

Trading Course

Web Designing

MSCIT Course

Shopping Business

Internet Business

Remotasks Course

Online Services

Top Sportsmans

Indian Army

Freedom Fighters

Top Scientists

Social Reformers

Motivational Speaker

Top Richest People

Join WhatsApp Group

Join Facebook Group

Like Facebook Page

PAN / Adhar / Licence Passport

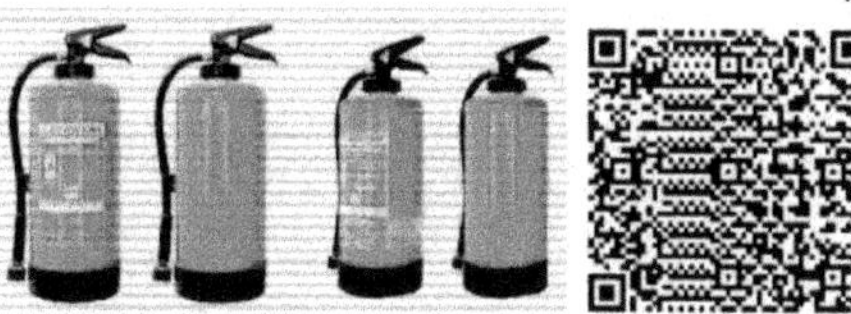

Fire extinguisher

Calliper

Hacksaw frame

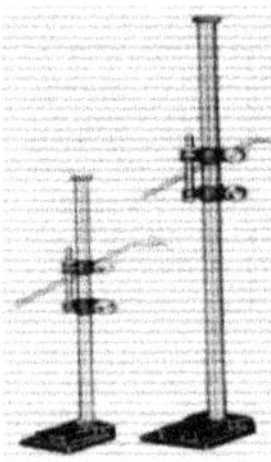

Universal surface guage

Hammer

Centre punch

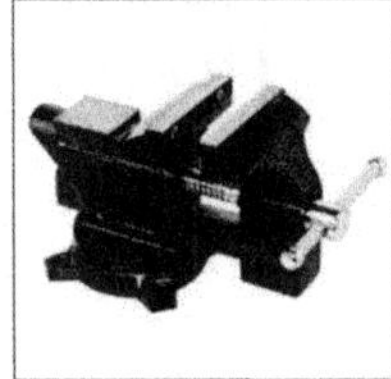

Bench vice

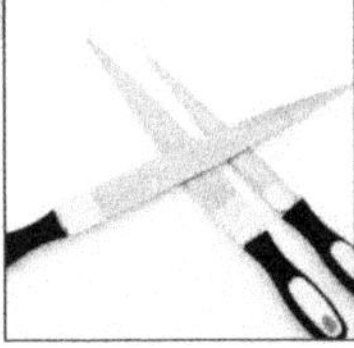

Files

Scraper

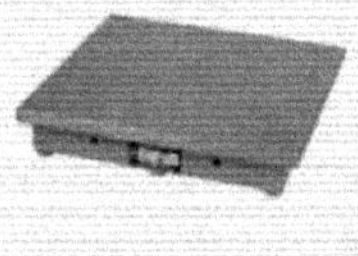

Surface Plate

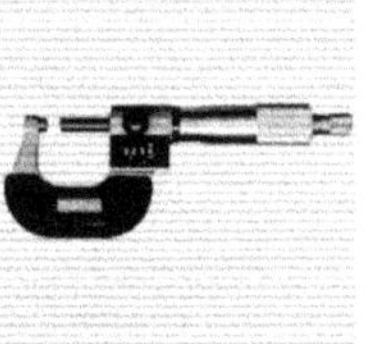

Outside Micrometer

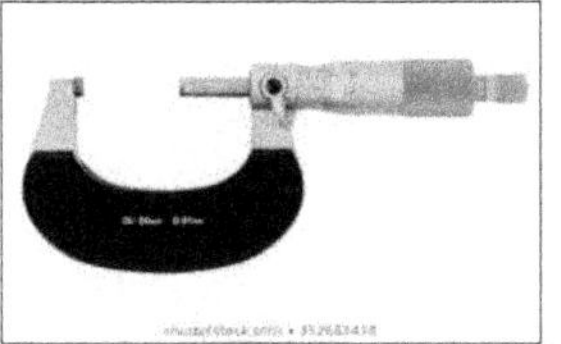

Micrometer

Depth micrometer

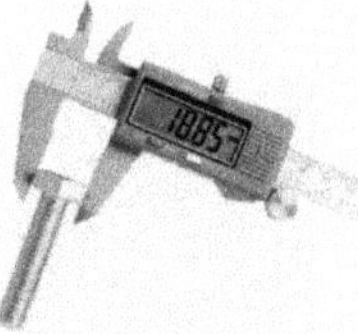

Vernier Calliper

Vernier bevel protractor

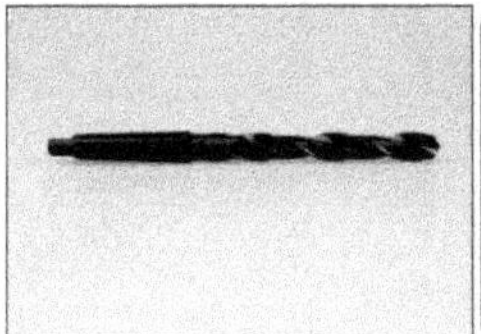

Drilling

Reamer

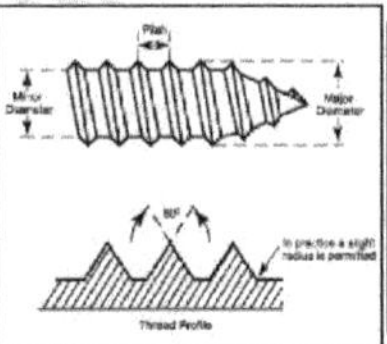

Thread

Tap Die

Grinding Wheel

Slip gauge

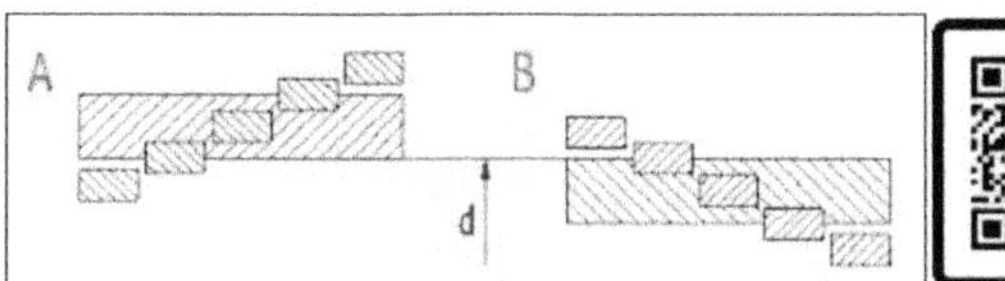

Limit fit tolerance

Lathe Machine

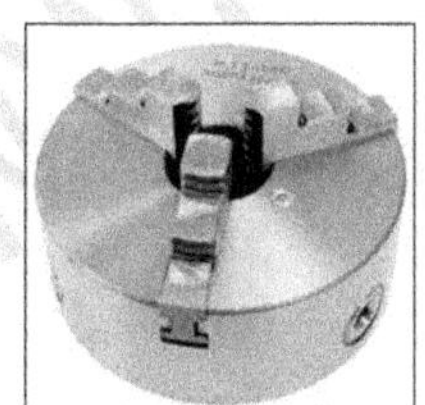

Lathe chuck

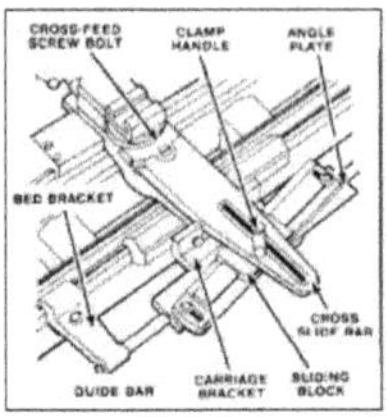

Taper turning attachment

taper ring gauge

screw pitch gauge

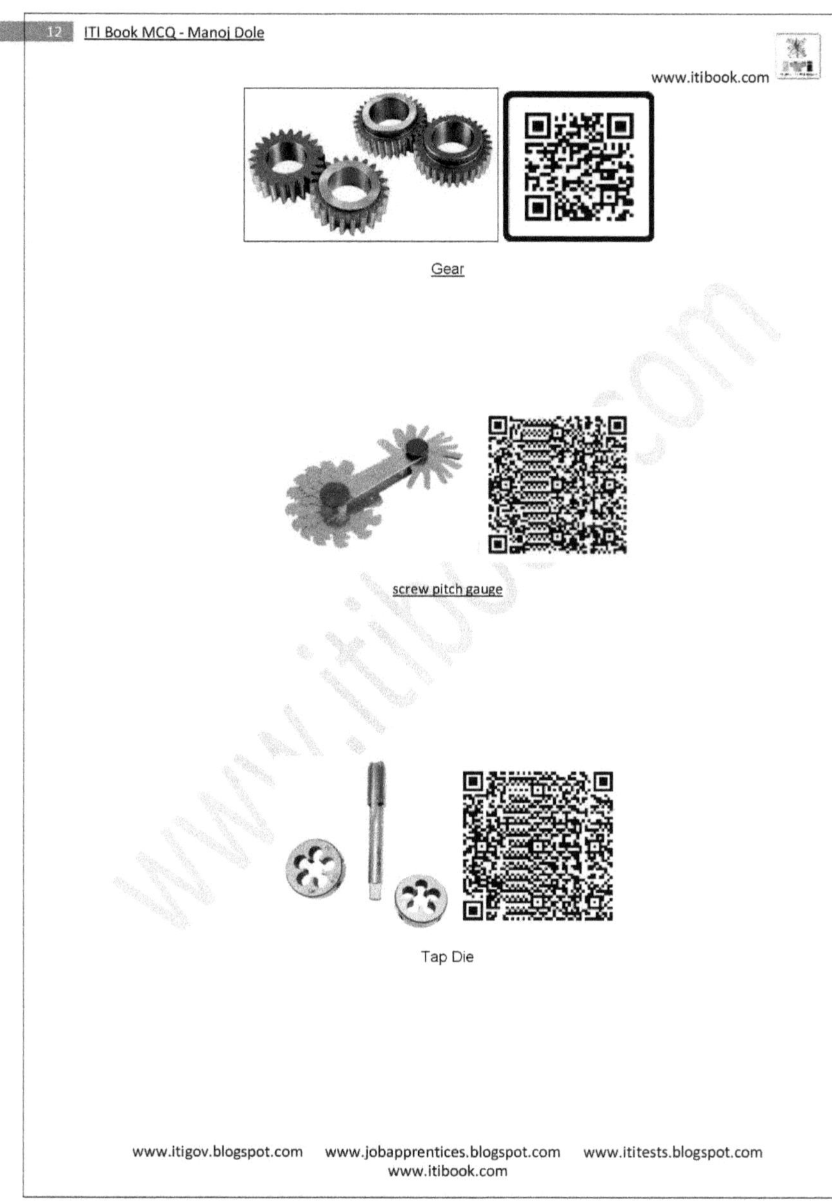
12
ITI Book MCQ - Manoj Dole
www.itibook.com
Gear
screw pitch gauge
Tap Die
www.itigov.blogspot.com www.jobapprentices.blogspot.com www.ititests.blogspot.com
www.itibook.com

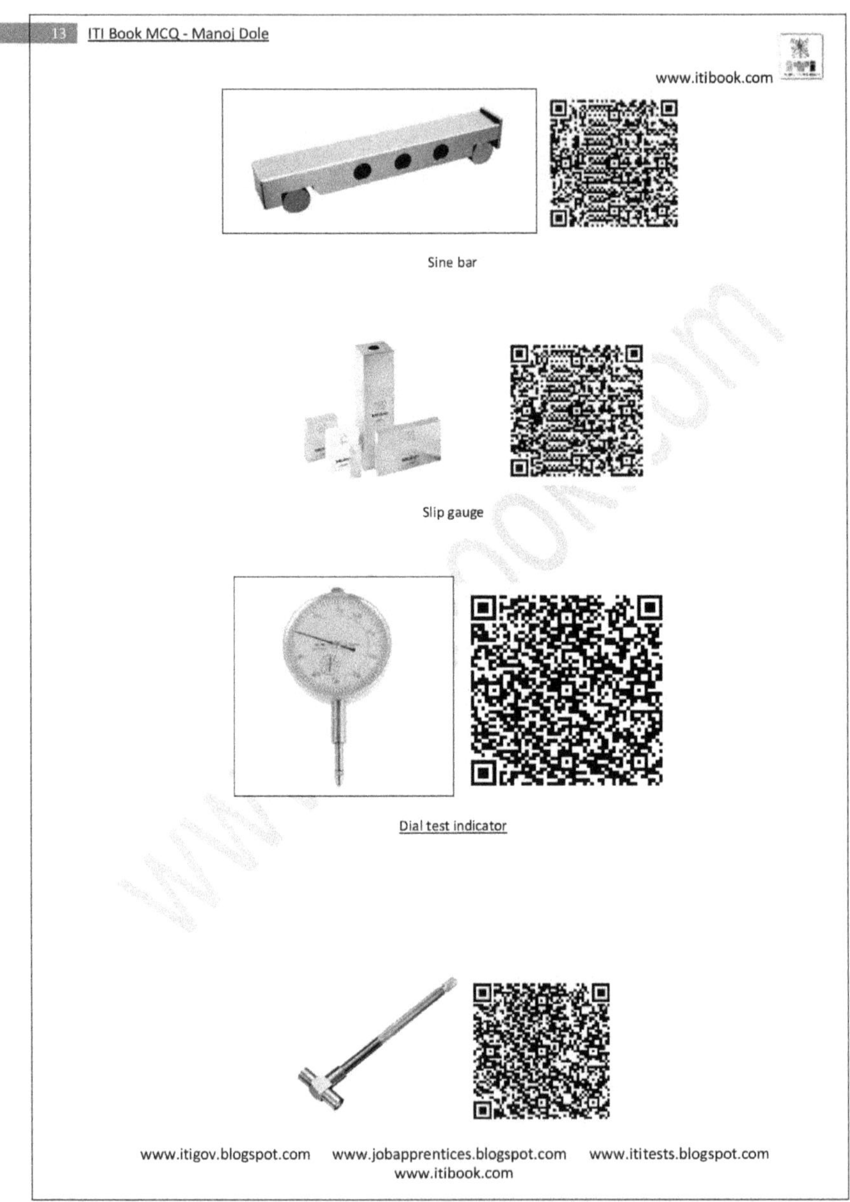
13 ITI Book MCQ - Manoj Dole
www.itibook.com
Sine bar
Slip gauge
Dial test indicator
www.itigov.blogspot.com www.jobapprentices.blogspot.com www.ititests.blogspot.com
www.itibook.com

14 ITI Book MCQ - Manoj Dole
www.itibook.com
Telescopic gauge
Feeler gauge
Centre gauge
Jig
www.itigov.blogspot.com www.jobapprentices.blogspot.com www.ititests.blogspot.com
www.itibook.com

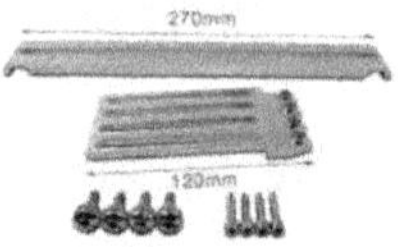

Fixture

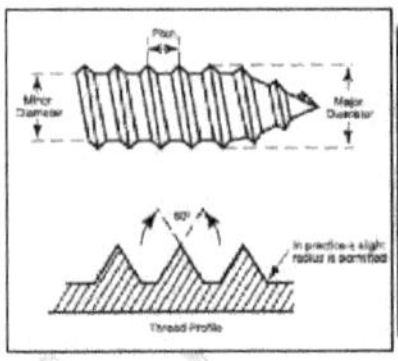

Thread

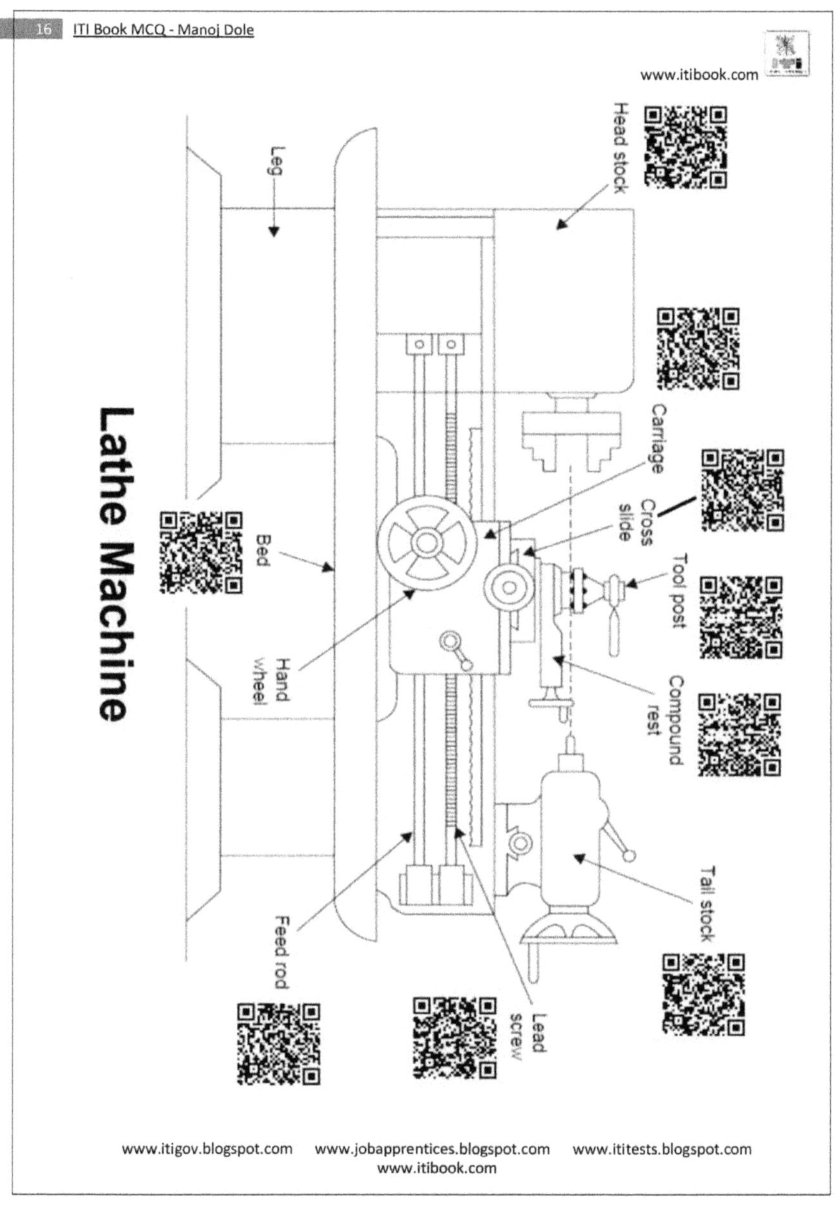
16 ITI Book MCQ - Manoj Dole
www.itibook.com
Lathe Machine
Head stock
Carriage
Cross slide
Tool post
Compound rest
Tail stock
Lead screw
Feed rod
Hand wheel
Bed
Leg
www.itigov.blogspot.com www.jobapprentices.blogspot.com www.ititests.blogspot.com
www.itibook.com

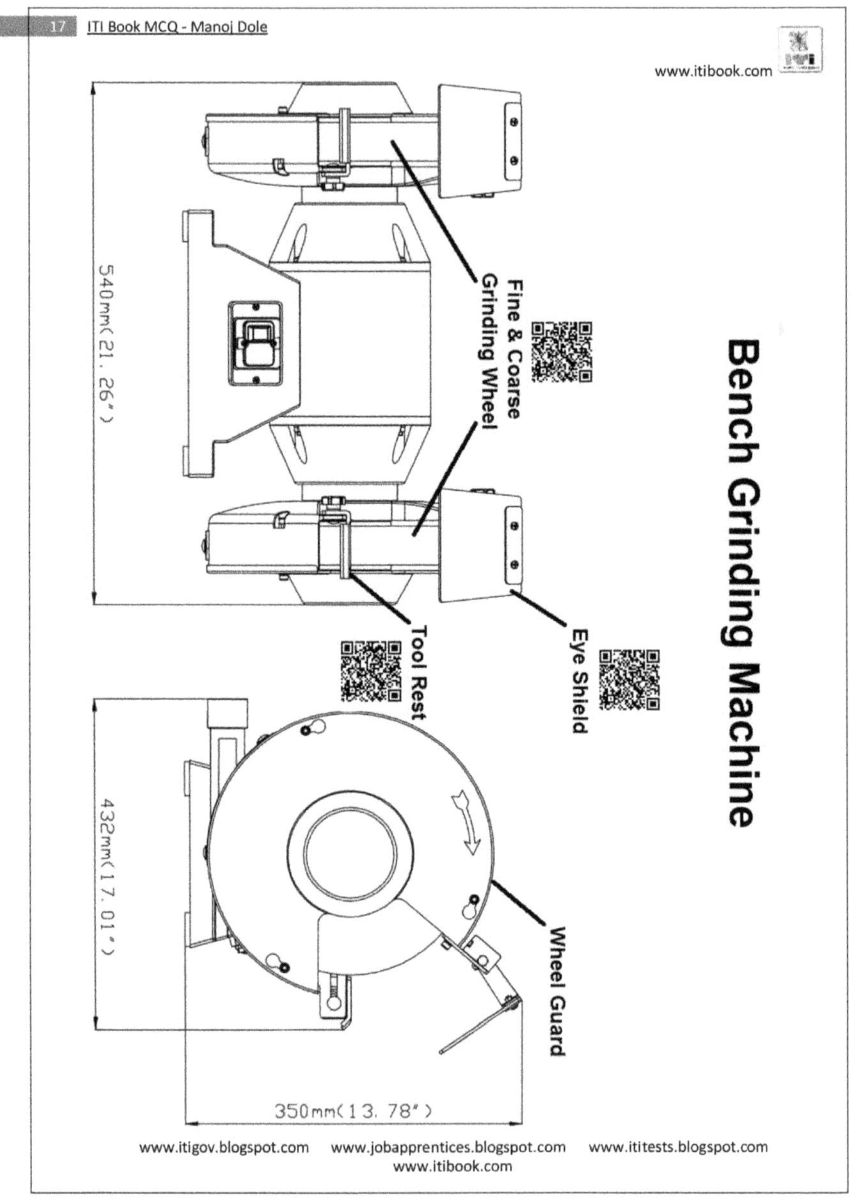
17 ITI Book MCQ - Manoj Dole
www.itibook.com
Bench Grinding Machine
Fine & Coarse Grinding Wheel
Eye Shield
Tool Rest
Wheel Guard
540mm(21. 26")
432mm(17. 01")
350mm(13. 78")
www.itigov.blogspot.com www.jobapprentices.blogspot.com www.ititests.blogspot.com
www.itibook.com

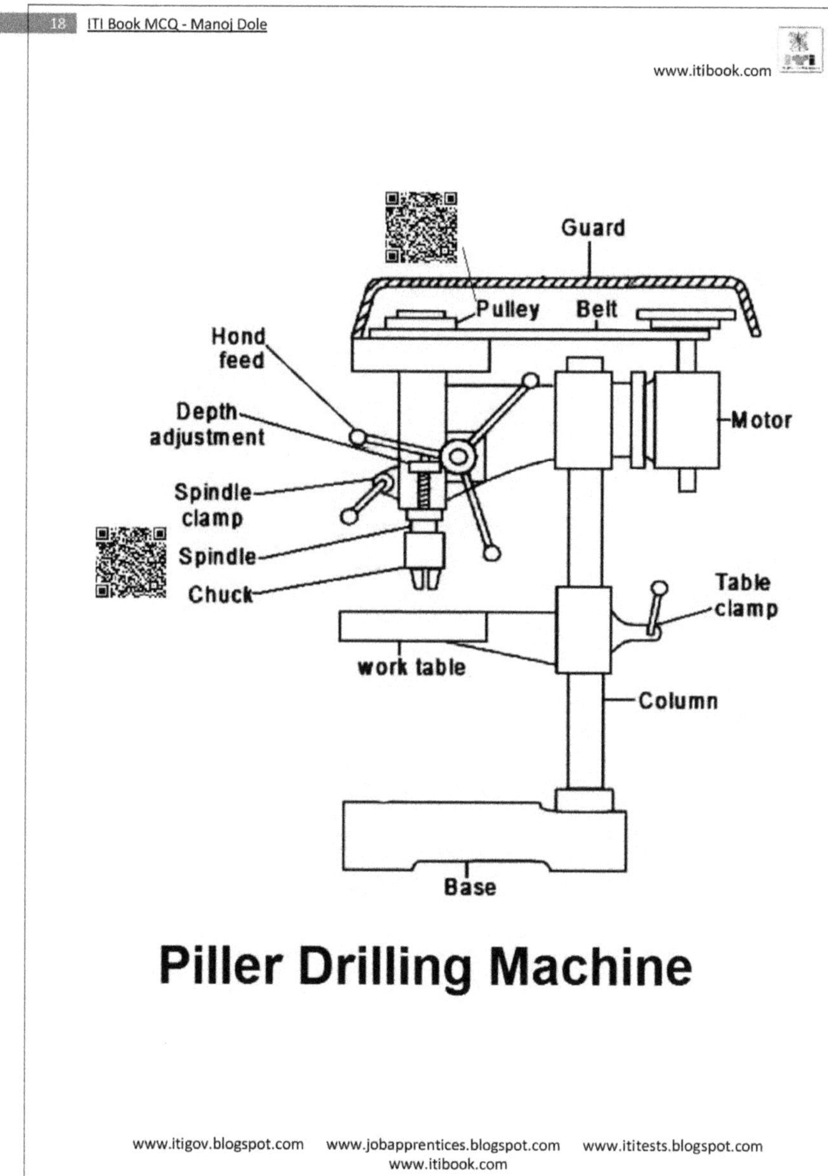
18
ITI Book MCQ - Manoj Dole
www.itibook.com
Guard
Pulley
Belt
Hond
feed
Depth
adjustment
Motor
Spindle
clamp
Spindle
Chuck
Table
clamp
work table
Column
Base
Piller Drilling Machine
www.itigov.blogspot.com
www.jobapprentices.blogspot.com
www.ititests.blogspot.com
www.itibook.com

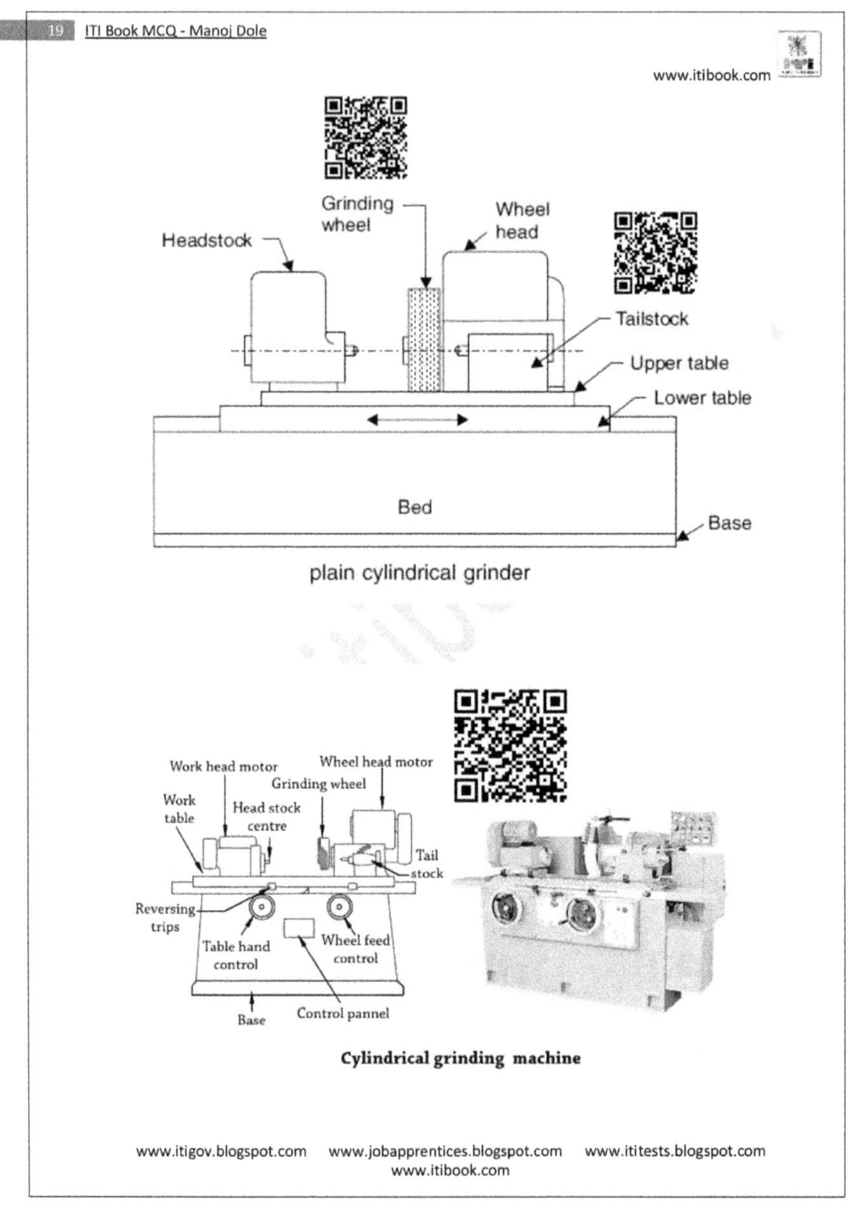
19 ITI Book MCQ - Manoj Dole
www.itibook.com
Grinding wheel
Wheel head
Headstock
Tailstock
Upper table
Lower table
Bed
Base
plain cylindrical grinder
Work head motor
Wheel head motor
Grinding wheel
Work table
Head stock centre
Tail stock
Reversing trips
Table hand control
Wheel feed control
Base
Control pannel
Cylindrical grinding machine
www.itigov.blogspot.com www.jobapprentices.blogspot.com www.ititests.blogspot.com
www.itibook.com

To study Different operations and parts of Surface Grinding Machine

SURFACE GRINDER

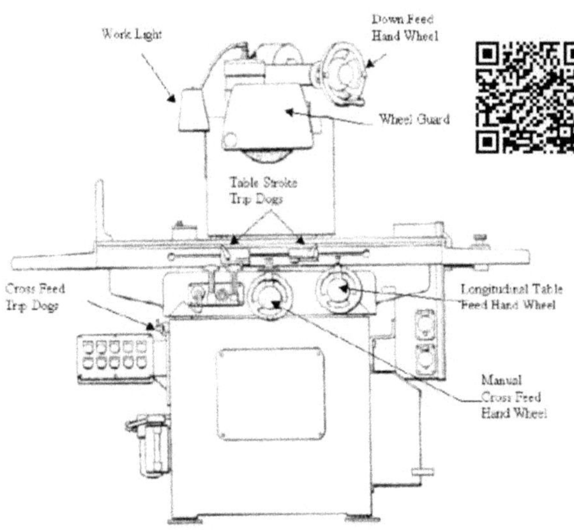

Surface grinding is used to produce a smooth finish on flat surfaces. It is a widely used abrasive machining process in which a spinning wheel covered in rough particles (grinding wheel) cuts

PLAIN OR HORIZONTAL MILLING MACHINE

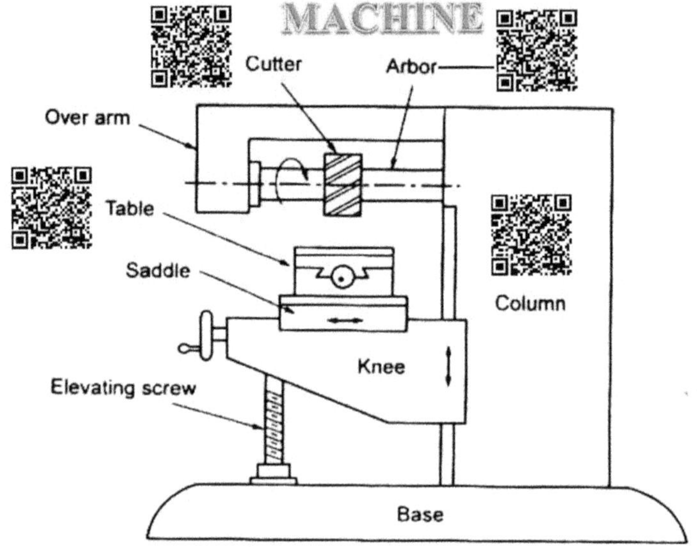

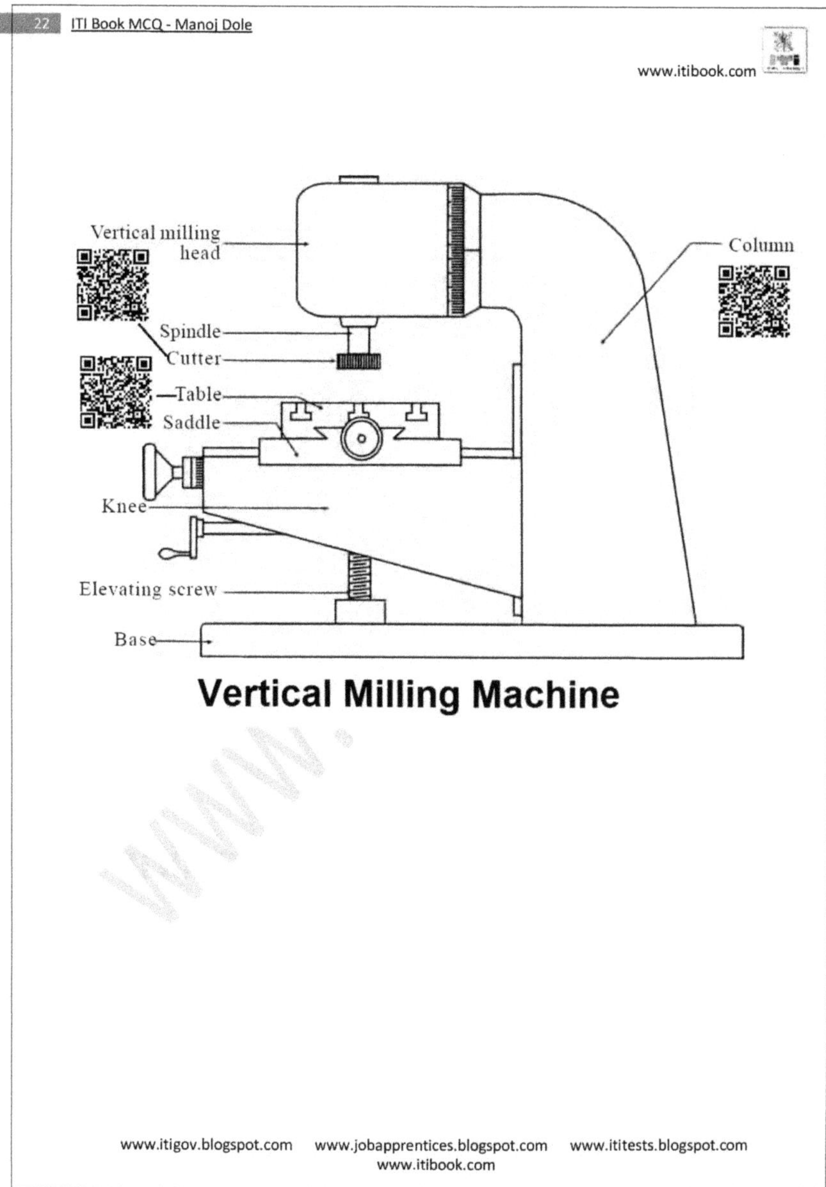

Vertical Milling Machine

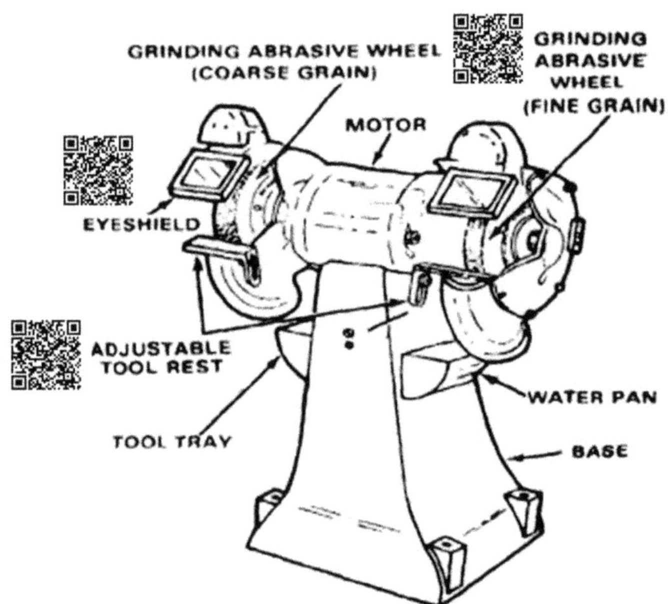

Pedastal Grinding Machine

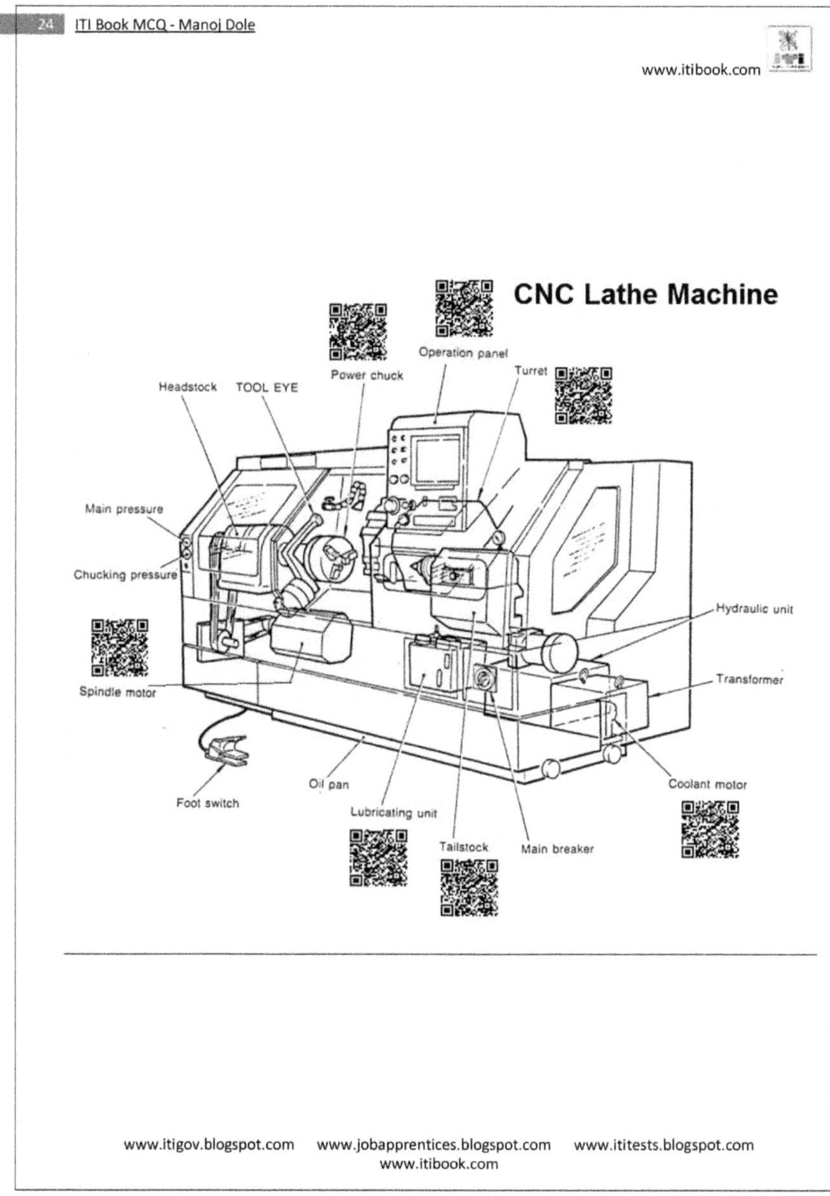
CNC Lathe Machine
Operation panel
Power chuck
Turret
Headstock
TOOL EYE
Main pressure
Chucking pressure
Hydraulic unit
Transformer
Spindle motor
Coolant motor
Oil pan
Foot switch
Lubricating unit
Tailstock
Main breaker

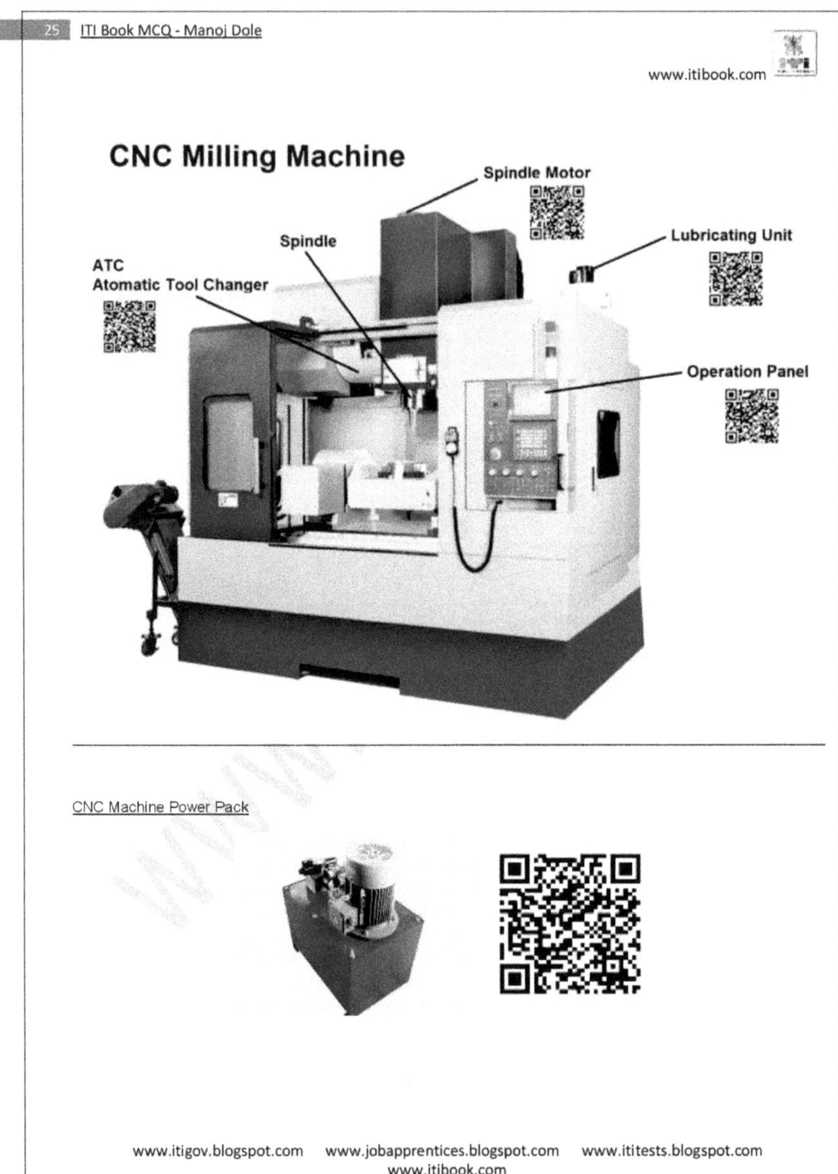
25
ITI Book MCQ - Manoj Dole
www.itibook.com
CNC Milling Machine
Spindle Motor
Spindle
Lubricating Unit
ATC
Atomatic Tool Changer
Operation Panel
CNC Machine Power Pack
www.itigov.blogspot.com www.jobapprentices.blogspot.com www.ititests.blogspot.com
www.itibook.com

Tool Change & Spindle Speed in CNC Machine.

Coolant in CNC Machine.

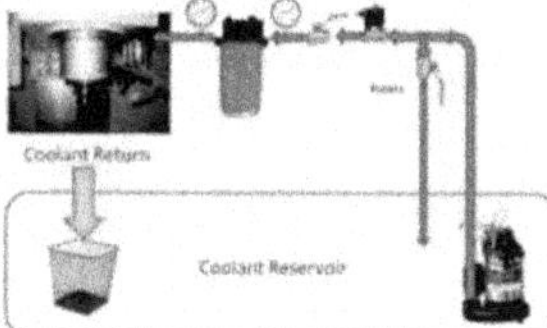

CHAPTER TWO

Machinist Second Year MCQ

01] The least count of a depth micrometer is -----------in metric system

A] 1mm

B] 0.001mm

C] 0.0001mm

D] 0.01mm

02] The pitch of the spindle of a depth micrometer is --------in metric pitch]

A] 0.01 mm

B] 0.02 mm

C] 0.3 mm

D] 0.5 mm

Types of Gauges

03] Which of the following statement is correct?'

A] Gauges are used to check the size

B] Template are used to chuck-the size

C] Gauges are used to measure the size

D] Gauges are used to check shape of component

04] At what standard temperature are the gauges kept in the section?

A] 100 C

B] 20° C

C] 100 F

D] 20° F

05] Which grade of slip gauge is generally used in workshop?
A] Grade 0
B] Grade 1
C] Grade H
D] Grade 0
06] The accuracy of a taper is generally checked by means of......
A] taper gauges
B] gauge blocks
C] indicator and height gauge
07] External tapers are checked with
A] limit plug gauge
B] taper ring gauge
C]taper plug gauge
D] thread plug gauge]
08] Threading tools are checked for accuracy for the 60◦ angle by using a
A] Thread plug gauge
B] centre gauge
C] screw pitch gauge
D] tool angle gauge
09] The number of threads per inch can be checked with a
A] tool gauge
B] metric rule by counting
C] ring gauge
D] screw pitch gauge

10] The accuracy of a taper is generally checked by means of......
A] taper gauges
B] gauge blocks
C] indicator and height gauge
11] External tapers are checked with
A] limit plug gauge
B] taper ring gauge
C]taper plug gauge
D] thread plug gauge]

12] Telescopic gauges are used to measure holes and slots]
A] from 10 mm to 100 mm
B] from 12 mm to 152 mm
C] from 12.7 mm to 152.4 mm
D] none of the above]
13] Small hole gauges are used to measure holes and slots]
A] below 10 mm
B] below 12.7 mm
C] below 20 mm
D] below 20.7 mm]

14] A set of number drill series consists of drills in the following ranges] Indicate the correct range

A] 1 to 40

B] 1 to 50

C] 1 to 80

D] 1 to 100

15] The feeler gauge is used for...

A] Checking surface roughness

B] Checking the redius of workpieces

C] Checking the gap between mating parts

D] Checking the accuracy of the hole locators

16] Generally gauges are made out of

A] nickel chromium

B] mild steel

C] cast steel

D] H.S.S.

17] Generally gauges are used for

A] mass production

B] measuring the components

C] individual component

D] checking the dimensional accuracy

18] A centre gauge is used to

A] check the pitch of the thread

B] set the tool at the correct centre height

C] check the fit of the thread

D] check the angle of the threading tool

19] A metric centre gauge has an angle of

A] 55°

B.60°

C] 47.5◦

D] 29◦

20] attachment is useful involving light machining.

A] Gear cutting attachment

B] Spherical turning attachment

C] Relieving attachment]

D] None of above

Cutter Grinding

21] Which one of the following is not an advantage of centre grinding?

A] Easier handling of the woe piece during loading and unloading

B] Handling of the longer work pieces

C] Both shaft and brittle work piece could be handled

D] Low grinding speed

22] Straight land surface is cut by tool and cutter grinder with-----------------

A] Plain wheel

B] Cup wheel

C] Conical wheel

D] Disc wheel

23] In grinding irregular, curved, tapered, convex and concave surfaces, the grinder used is ~

A] Cylindrical grinder

B] Internal grinder

C] Surface grinder

D] Tool & Cutter grinder]

24] Which type of grinding machine Is used for sharpening of tool is milling cutters/drills/hobs/broaches?

A] Chucking]

B] Tool and cutter

C] Centre less

D] Bench

25] Which type of grinding wheel is used on tool and cutter grinder to sharpen the milling cutter?

A] Straight cup wheel

B] Flaring cup wheel

C] Dish wheel

D] Saucer wheel

26] ....is used on tool and cutter Grinders mainly to sharpen milling cutters and reamers

A] Straight cup

B] Haring cup

C] Dish

D] Recessed both sides

27] When using a diamond wheel for cutter grinding, a wheel speed of 1600/mm is recommended] What should be the depth of cut?]

A] 0.005-0.025mm

B] 0.025-0.04mm

C] 0.04-0.05mm

D] 0.05-0.05mm

28] Which of the following is precision grinding machine?

A] Pedestal grinding machine

C] Cylindrical surface and Tool & Cutter grinding machine

B] Bench grinding machine

D] Hand grinding machine

29] TOOl and cutter are re-shaped by -------------

A] Surface grinding machine

B] tool and cutter grinding machine

C] Cylindrical grinding machine

D] Rotary grinding machine

30] Name the part of a tool and cutter grinder on which wheel head is being mounted]

A] Base

B] Saddle

C] Column

D] Table

31] The error due to faulty centre holes are eliminated by operation of -------

A] Surface grinder

B] centre-less grinder

C] Tool and cutter grinder

D] Cylindrical grinder

32] In centre less grinding, the work piece rest on -----

A] Centre of the chuck

B] Face plate

C] Rest blade

D] Ali of these

33] Which type of grinding machine Is used for sharpening of miilingtools?

A] Chucking]

B] Tool and cutter

C] Centre less

D] Bench

34] For re-sharpening of milling cutter in tool and cutter grinder, which one is suitable size grinding wheel?

A] .35 grit size of grinding wheel

B] 46 grit size of grinding wheel

C] 60 grit size of grinding wheel

D] 80 grit size of grinding wheel

Depth micrometer

35] Least count of depth micrometer is

A] 0.5 mm

B] 0.2 mm

C] 0.001 mm

D] 0.01 mm

36] A micrometer has a positive error of 0.02 mm] What is the correct reading when the micrometer measures 25.41 mm?

A] 25.37 mm

B] 25.39 mm

C] 25.43 mm

D] 25.45 mm

37] in which one of the following micrometer the graduations on thimble and sleeve are in reverse direction to that of outside micrometer?

A] Inside micrometer

B] Depth micrometer

C] Tube micrometer

D] Flange micrometer

38] Micrometer works on the principle of ------

A] Screw

B] Bolt

C] Stud

D] Nut & Screw

39] The smallest inside micrometer has the graduation marked on the sleeve

A] 10mm

B] 12mm

C] 13mm

D] 25mm

40] The graduations of a depth micrometer is ----------

A] in the reverse direction to that of the outside micrometer both thimble and sleeves

B] In the reverse direction only of the sleeve

C] In the reverse direction only on the thimble

D] Similar to an outside micrometer

41] usefulforcutting splines etc.

A] Gear cutting attachment

B] Spherical turning attachment

C] Relieving attachment]

D] None of above

42] The angle between the intersecting axes of mating gears.

A] Addendum angle

B] Dedendurn angle

C] Shaft angle

D] Root angle

43] The angle between the axis and the root surface of a tooth space.

A] Addendum angle

B] Dedendurn angle

C] Shaft angle

D] Root angle

44] The angle between the pitch cone generator and the tip surface of the tooth.

A] Addendum angle

B] Dedendurn angle

C] Shaft angle

D] Root angle

45] The angle between the pitch cone generator and the root surface of the tooth.

A] Addendum angle

B] Dedendurn angle

C] Shaft angle

D] Root angle

46] It is the sum of the pitch cone angles of the mating gears]

A] Addendum angle

B] Dedendurn angle

C] Shaft angle

D] Root angle

Gears

47] Used in milling machine, shaping machine and lathe for transmitting power

A] Straight tooth bevel gear

B] Miter bevel gear

C] Angular bevel gear

D] Spiral bevel gear

48] Advantage of using this is for smooth running and high speed range
A] Straight tooth bevel gear
B] Miter bevel gear
C] Angular bevel gear
D] <u>Spiral bevel gear</u>
49] Used to connects shafts which are at an angle but not intersecting
B] Miter bevel gear
C] Angular bevel gear
D] Spiral bevel gear
E] <u>Hypoid bevel gear</u>
50] Used in automobile drives]
B] Miter bevel gear
C] Angular bevel gear
D] Spiral bevel gear
E] <u>Hypoid bevel gear</u>
51]] What is template?
A] One of the cutting operation
B] One of the form turning
C] <u>same figure of the job</u>
D] one of the tool
52] Which purpose use template?
A] <u>For marking & checking</u>
B] for threading
C] for turning
D] for measuring
53] Which material is use for making template?
A] H.C.S] plate
B] Special tool steel
C] brass or copper

d] G.I] sheet or M.S] thin sheet

54] ---------------is used for checking shape of component

A] Template

B] Snap gauge

C] Instrument

D] Sine bar

55] For face copying........] Type template is used

A] Rounded

B] Plate type

C] Flat

D] Triangular

Types of milling machines

56] Spindle is perpendicular to the work table

A] Horizontal milling machine

B] Vertical milling machine

C] Universal milling machine]

D] Lathe machine

Verticle milling machine

57] The table can be swivelled in horizontal plane

A] Horizontal milling machine

B] Vertical milling machine

C] Universal milling machine]

D] Lathe machine

58] The spindle is horizontal to the work table

A] Horizontal milling machine

B] Vertical milling machine

C] Universal milling machine]

D] Lathe machine
59] Rigid, sturdy and accommodates heavy work
A] Horizontal milling machine
B] Vertical milling machine
C] Universal milling machine]
D] Lathe machine
60] Boring, keyway cutting, profile milling can be done on this machine
A] Horizontal milling machine
B] Vertical milling machine
C] Universal milling machine]
D] Lathe machine
61] Helical grooves and gears can be milled on this machine.
A] Horizontal milling machine
B] Vertical milling machine
C] Universal milling machine]
D] Lathe machine
62] Slide movement on the column
A] Longitudinal feed
B] Cross feed
C] Vertical feed
D] Circular feed]
63] Slide movements on the knee
A] Longitudinal feed
B] Cross feed
C] Vertical feed
D] Circular feed]
64] Rotary table
A] Longitudinal feed
B] Cross feed
C] Vertical feed
D] Circular feed]
65] Table traverse]
A] Longitudinal feed
B] Cross feed
C] Vertical feed
D] Circular feed]

Reamer

66] This reamer is used where finish is not very critical.

A] Solid fluted machine reamer
B] Chucking reamer
C] Rose reamer
D] Shell reamer

67] Several sizes of this reamers are handled with one shank]
A] Solid fluted machine reamer
B] Chucking reamer
C] Rose reamer
D] Shell reamer
68] Similar to hand reamer either with straight/left hand helix.
A] Solid fluted machine reamer
B] Chucking reamer
C] Rose reamer
D] Shell reamer
69] Similar to jobber reamer but with 'shorter and deeper flutes.
A] Solid fluted machine reamer
B] Chucking reamer
C] Rose reamer
D] Shell reamer
70] Other name of this is Jobber reamer]
A] Solid fluted machine reamer
B] Chucking reamer
C] Rose reamer
D] Shell reamer
71] This reamer is designed to cut on its end]
A] Solid fluted machine reamer
B] Chucking reamer
C] Rose reamer
D] Shell reamer

72] A short reamer with an axial hole used with an arbor or mandrel is called -------

A] Parallel reamer

B] Adjustable reamer

C] Expansion reamer

<u>D] Chucking reamer</u>

73] Which one of the following machine reamers is used to correct the misalignment between the reamer axis and the work axis?

<u>A] Floating blade reamer</u>

B] Machine jig reamer]

C] Shell reamer

D] Chucking reamer

74] The reamer is used for...

A] Drilling holes in thin sheets

B] Drilling deep holes

C] Removing burrs

D] <u>Enlarging and finishing holes</u>

75] The reamer teeth are unevenly spaced because...

A] They are easy to manufacture

B] <u>They can reduce chattering</u>

C] They help to cut metal gradually

D] They help to remove the reamer easily

76] Which among the following is not a capability of reamers?

A] Finishing small holes

B] <u>Finishing any machined profiles</u>

C] Accuracy to closer limits

D] Producing high quality surface finish

<u>Drilling & Drilling machines</u>

77] The taper shank drills are held on the machine by means of...

A] Chucks

<u>B] Sleeves</u>

C] Drift

D] Vice

78] Drill chucks are fitted on the drilling machine spindle by means of a...

A] Knurled ring

<u>B] Arbor</u>

C] Drift

D] Pinion and key

79] The Morse taper provided on drills ranges between...

A] MT 1 to MT 5

B] MT 1 to MT 4

C] MT 0 to MT 5

D] MT 0 to MT 4

80] A drift is used for...

A] Drawing a drill location

B] Fixing chuck on the machine spindle

C] Removing a broken drill from the work

D] Removing the drill from the machine spindle

81] When the taper shank of the drill is larger than the machine spindle, the device to hold the drill is a...

A] Drill sleeve

B] Taper socket

C] Drill drift

D] Chuck and key

82] The suitable cutting fluid for drilling mild steel in a drilling machine is...

A] Synthetic soluble oil

B] Neat oil

C] Distilled water

D] Soluble oil

83] A special feature of the radial drilling machine is...

A] It can be used for drilling with a H.S.S] drill

B] Table can be moved and set at any position

C] A variety of speeds is available

D] The spindle can be brought to any position

84] The point angle of drills depends on...

A] The size of the drill

B] The type of machine

C] The material of the work

D] The RPM of the drill

85] The point angle for a standard drill is...

A] 60°

B] 108°

C] 118°

D] 135°

86] The helical angle determines the...

A] Cutting angle

B] Chew angle

C] Rake angle

D] Lip angle

87] The clearance angle of the drill is between...

A] 3◦ to 5◦

B] 8◦ to 12◦

C] 12◦ to 20◦

D] 15◦ to 20◦

88] In a remote place (no electricity available] a rail track is to be drilled] Choose the right drilling machine

A] Radial drilling machine

B] Pillar drilling machine

C] Ratchet drilling machine

D] Sensitive drilling Machine

89] A drilling machine used by a carpenter for cabinet making is a...

A] Ratchet drilling machine

B] Radial drilling machine

C] Breast drilling machine

D] Sensitive drilling machine

90] Which one of the following drilling machines is used for drilling holes where electricity is not available?

A] Bench drilling machine

B] Pillar drilling machine

C] Redial drilling machine

D] Ratchet drilling machine

91] Which one of the following drilling machine is used for heavy duty work?

A] Bench drilling machine

B] Pillar drilling machine

C] Radial drilling machine

D] Electric hand drilling machine

92] Drill chuck are held on the machine spindle by means of ------

A] arbor

B] Drift

C] draw-in bar

D] Chuck nut

93] Different speeds are obtained in a sensitive bench drilling machine by ----

A] Belt pulley mechanism

B] Hydraulic mechanism

C] Rack and Pinion mechanism

D] Cam and follower mechanism

94] The alternator in a car delivers 4A and has a load of 3 ohms connected across its terminals] Find the voltage of the circuit

A] 18V

B] 24V

C] 12V

D] 16V

95] A voltage source produces an IR drop of 40V across a 20 ohms resistance, 60V across a 30 ohms resistance and 180V across a 90 ohms resistance all in series] How much is the applied voltage?

A] 180 V

B] 240 V

C] 100 V

D] 280 V

96] How big is the peak amplitude of a sine-wave with an effective value of 220 volts?

A] 311 V

B] 380 V

C] 400 V

D] 440 V

97] The peak-to-peak voltage is 99V] how big is the effective value of the sine wave?

A] 70 V

B] 44.5V

C] 49.5 V

D] 35 V

98] A moving coil voltmeter reads 10 V AC] How big is the effective voltage?

A] higher

B] lower

C] the same

D] 10% higher

99] A moving iron ammeter reads 10 A] how big is the peak current of the oscillation?

A] 7.07 A

B] 1.1414A

C] 70.7 A

D] 14.1 A

100] A current of 2 amps flows through a resistance of 10 ohms] The power dissipated in the resistance is equal to...

A] 20 watts

B] 200 watts

C] 40 watts

D] 5 watts

101] Power companies are interested in improving the power factor to

A] reduce line current

B] increase motor efficiency

C] increase volt-amperes

D] decrease power

102] Moving coil instrument works on the effect of...

A] chemical effect

B] heating effect

C] electrostatic effect

D] electromagnetic effect

CNC Machine Tape Punch

image

103] Tape punch having 1 inch in width tape it is made by

A] Paper Mylar

B] Aluminum Mylar

C] Plastic

D] Above all

104] In point two point positioning positioning system........] Is acceptable

A] Open loop control system

B] Closed loop control system

C] Above both

D] None of them

105] In CNC machine having.......

A] Lead screw

B] Ball lead screw

C] Above both

D] None of both

CNC Program Coordinate

image

106] The aim of sub program is........

A] For find coordinates X Y Z.

B] For other small machine.

C] To avoid cutting tool nose tool nose penetration in Jobs surface of high speed.

D] While machining of job in special condition do not use time to time of program block.

107] What is mean by while while xyz co-ordinate point measure zero-measurement

A] Reference mark.

B] Work zero

C] Co-ordinate points

D] Above all

108] CNC machine specified by axis......

A] 2 axis

B] 3 axis

C] 4 axis

D] Above all

CNC Machine Axis

image

109] Xyz axis of CNC machines which point is used for measurements.

A] Work zero point

B] Machine zero point

C] Common zero point

D] Above all

110] Following which point is not useful in CNC machine.

A] various operation done on CNC machine.

B] Less amount for inspection.

C] Hard for setting measure.

D] Machine efficiency is depend upon operators skill.

111] For selection of zero offset before necessary..........

A] cutter is fixed on machine table.

B] The data entered in machine.

C] Job is fixed on machine table.

D] Speed and feed selection necessary before machine operates.

CNC Work Zero Offset Setting.

image

112] In zero offset program indicates........] Code of following

A] X y z

B] X0 y0 z00

C] X10 Y20 Z30

D] G71

113] Work zero is

A] Datum of machine zero on job position.

B] Indicate by X0Y0Z0.

C] Selection of point on job according to program.

D] The end of machining point

114] M command is used for starting operation and complete revolution cycle M03 means.

A] Stop the program.

B] Program completed and reset.

C] Complete the program.

D] Spindle clockwise motion.

CNC Machine Power Pack

image

115] CNC machine is not manually operated it is control by...........

A] Program

B] operation

C] Cam

D] Plug board system

116] In CNC machine M13 means

A] coolant stop

B] coolant on

C] spindle stop

D] coolant on & spindle on

117] The function of power pack in CNC machine.

A] For balancing of lubricants heat.

B] For increasing heat of lubricants.

C] For destroy heat of lubricant.

D] Above all.

CNC Machine Bed.

image

118] The section of CNC machine bed is.....

A] Flat

B] Half round

C] Rectangular

D] Triangular

119] Following which statement is disadvantage of CNC machine.

A] Less inspection charge.

B] Less tooling charge.

C] Increase production rate.

D] High establishment charge.

120] The point to point system is more effective for......

A] Turning

B] Profile milling

C] Grinding

D] Drilling

Tool Setting on NC Machine.

image

121] Tool setting on NC machine on......] unit.

A] Presetting device.

B] Order special device without machine.

C] On n c machine other empty time.

D] When other operation working on machine.

122] For measuring system having built-in coordinates in this system..........] is called zero position.

A] Reference point.

B] Machine zero point.

C] Work zero point

D] Program zero point.

123] Job turning on CNC machine 50 mm dia turn with programs said the trial run 50.1 mm at production time following which Idea used for correct dia making

A] by increase offset of tool 0.1 mm.

B] by increase offset of tool 0.05 mm

C] by decrease offset of tool 0.05 mm

D] by decrease offset of tool 0.1 mm

CNC Copying Lathe Machine.

image

124] For measure zero offset dim dimensions on CNC machine.........mode is set

A] MDI

B] Jog

C] Automatic

D] preset

125] Coping unit of copying lathe is work on

A] Mechanical power system

B] Hand power system

C] Hydraulic power system

D] None of them

126] One of the below miscellaneous function used in CNC program for coolant on

A] M08

B] M09

C] M10

D] M11

Clamping the Job on CNC Machine.

clamping the job on cnc.jpg

127] One of the below miscellaneous function in CNC program used for coolant off

A] M11

B] M10

C] M9

D] M15

128] In CNC program which miscellaneous function used for clamping the job on machine table.

A] M09

B] M10

C] M11

D] M15

129] One of the below miscellaneous function in CNC program used for unclamp the job

A] M11

B] M15

C] M30

D] M60

Work piece change in CNC Machine.

workpice change in cnc.jpg

130] In CNC program which miscellaneous function used for change of workpiece

A] M30

B] M60

C] M68

D] M78

131] The machine is.........for zero off-setting on CNC Machine.

A] In MDI Mode

B] In JOG Mode

C] In Automatic Mode

D] In Present Mode

132] The feed rate on NC Machine is indicate by ......code.

A] X

B] Y

C] F

D] Z

CNC Machine Axis Position]

cnc machine axis position.jpg

133] The position of axis is indicate by.......code.

A] X,Y,Z

B] P,Q,R

C] A,B,C

D] M,N,O

134] CNC Drilling Machine is on.......Axis Programmed.

A] Two Axis

B] Three Axis

C] Four Axis

D] Six Axis

135] From.......unit collect instruction in control unit of CNC

A] Machine Tool

B] Instruction

C] Magnetic Box

D] Memory

Working Graph of CNC Machine]

136] For preparing tape of NC Machine----------code is used.

A] EIA Code

B] ISO Code

C] ASC Code

D] None of them.

137] CNC Machine gives more accurate production than convention machine, But it is more expensive because.

A] It has AC cabin

B] It has dust proof cabin

C] It has strong foundation

D] It has more space

138] CNC Machine is working on graphical base the point on digital line, indicated digital points call..........

A] Graph

B] Input Media

C] Co-Ordinate

D] Original Point

Axis Rotary Motion in CNC Machine]

axis rotary motion in CNC.png

139] On CNC Machine for longitudinal feed has.......axes, cross feed......axis and for vertical feed........axis name given.

A] A,B,C
B] X,Y,Z
C] P,Q,R
D] M,N,O
140] For rotary motion CNC machine axis has.......name given.
A] A,B,C
B] X,Y,Z
C] P,Q,R
D] M,N,O
141] CNC Machine means.......
A] Natural Control Machine
B] Pneumatic control Machine
C] Numerical Control Machine
D] No Command Machine
142] Following which advantage of Pneumatic power system
A] For increase production rate.
B] Less cash for layout
C] Good climate for work
D] Above all
Principle of CNC Machine Templates.

image

143] For face copying........] Type template is used
A] Rounded
B] Plate type
C] Flat
D] Triangular
144]............] Is Main principle of CNC MACHINE?
A] Indicate all states in numbers
B] More time required for mechanical control on machine.
C] Cutting speed is more than manual control.

D] Production sequence in workshop is stored by block number in machine.

145] For copy of one shaft.......] Type template is used.

A] Rounded

B] Triangular

C] Flats

D] Square

CNC Program Tool Path.

image

146] The symptoms of continuous path is

A] Called counting system.

B] Tool and work piece on co-ordinate Axis for inter related motion.

C] By the setting of cutter feed and speed

D] Above all

147] Misc command M30 means........

A] End of program and reset

B] Program stop

C] Clockwise motion of spindle

D] Complete the programs

148] Following which affect on milling surface while by milling with unsetting spindle vertical milling machine with- longitudinal feed.

A] Convex surface

B] Concave surface

C] Radius cross line

D] Rough surface

CNC Milling Operation]

image

149] While milling by vertical milling machine with 12 mm dia end mill cutter through slot provide on mild steel plate the cutter is sleep and broken for this fault how it is avoid.

A] High speed spindle

B] Low cutting speed

C] Increase of cut depth

D] Less the depth and feed of cutter

150] Having 5 mm pitch of screw and dividing ratio of 40 : 1 what is lead of milling machine

A] 0.25 mm

B] 5 mm

C] 8 mm

D] 200 mm

151] If not use of backlash Eliminator slap cutter used for down milling operation which safety to be observed?

A] Less lead and depth

B] High lead

C] high lead and less depth

D] High lead and high speed

CNC Machine Zero & Feed Rate.

cnc machine zero.PNG

152] Zero offset is the distance between.....] And.........

A] G41 & g42

B] Machine zero & work zero

C] Reference point and tapping mode

D] None of them

153] The feed rate is programmed as mm per minute with G ....] And mm per- Revolution with G.

A] G41 & g42

B] G 43 and G 40

C] G 94 and g95

D] None of them

154] For collection all instructions from.......] In CNC control unit

A] Memory

B] Tape reader

C] Control panel

D] Operator

CNC Drilling Machine.

cnc drilling machine.jpg

155] For control forward and backward of- CNC drilling machine y axis.........

A] Spindle

B] Table

C] Clockwise

D] Column

156] M 01 command means.....

A] For stopping programs

B] End of program and reset

C] Stopping programs condition

D] Clockwise rotation of machine spindle

157] CNC machine is founded by American scientist john person in.......] Year

A] 1950

B] 1952

C] 1955

D] 1957

CNC Control, Input & Memory Unit.

cnc control.jpg

158] Name of unit used to command the CNC machine.

A] Control unit

B] Memory unit

C] Input unit

D] Output unit

159] Name of unit used to processing the data in CNC machine.

A] Memory unit

B] Control unit

C] Input unit

D] Output unit

160] Name of unit used to storing the data in CNC machine.

A] Input unit

B] Control unit

C] Memory unit

D] Output unit

Servo Motor in CNC Machine.

servo motor.jpg

161] Name of unit used to calculation of data in CNC machine.

A] Output unit

B] Arithmetic unit

C] Memory unit

D] Input unit

162] Name of unit used to display result of processing data in CNC machine

A] Arithmetic unit

B] Output unit

C] Memory unit

D] Input unit

163] Servo Motor in CNC machine is used to..............

A] Changing tool on machine spindle

B] Driving machine spindle

C] Fixing job on machine spindle

D] Proving job on spindle

Types of CNC Machine.

types of cnc.jpg

164] One of the below part of CNC machine used to changing tools on spindle.

A] Servo Motor

B] Control panel

C] Automatic tool changer A T C

D] High speed spindle

165] One of the below CNC machine in CNC milling category is.......

A] Chucking centre

B] CNC late

C] Vertical machining centre

D] Surface grinding machine

166] One of the below CNC machine in turning centre or CNC lathe category is.......

A] Vertical machining centre

B] Horizontal machining centre

C] Vertical turning centre

D] Profile grinding machin

Miscellaneous Functions for CNC Machine.

miscellaneous function.jpg

167] One of the below CNC machine in grinding Centre category is.....

A] Universal milling centre

B] Cylindrical grinding machine

C] CNC late
D] Vertical machining centre
168] In CNC Machine programming word M indicates
A] Feed rate
B] Spindle speed
C] Miscellaneous function
D] Tool number
169] In CNC Machine programming preparatory function G00 is for.....
A] Linear interpolation
B] Clockwise circular interpolation
C] Counter clockwise circular interpellation
D] Hold

Preparatory Functions for CNC Machine.

preparatory function.jpg

170] In CNC Machine programming preparatory function G02 is for.....
A] Linear interpolation
B] Clockwise circular interpolation
C] Counter clockwise circular interpellation
D] Hold
171] One of the bellow preparatory function G 00 is used in CNC program for.........
A] Linear interpellation or feed motion in straight line.
B] Clockwise circular interpellation
C] Point to point Positioning or Rapid motion.
D] Counter clockwise circular interpellation
172] One of the bellow preparatory function used in CNC program for 3D interpellation
A] G 05
B] G12

C] G17

D] G18

Threading & Tapping on CNC Machine.

threading & tapping on cnc.jpg

173] One of the bellow preparatory you function used in CNC program for thread cutting constant lead

A] G33

B] G40

C] G53

D] G62

174] One of the bellow preparatory function used in CNC program for tapping operation.

A] G-40

B] G53

C] G62

D] G63

175] One of the below preparatory function used in CNC program for milling operation.

A] G62

B] G63

C] G 78, 79

D] G81

Drilling, Boring & Reaming on CNC Machine

drilling boring & reaming.jpg

176] One of the bellow preparatory function used in CNC program for drilling operation.

A] G 81

B] G 82

C] G 84

D] G 85

177] One of the bellow preparatory function used in CNC program for reaming operation.

A] G 84

B] G 85

C] G 86

D] G 90

178] One of the below preparatory function used in CNC program for boring operation.

A] G 86

B] G 90

C] G 91

D] G 92

CNC Program Sequence Number.

cnc program sequence.png

179] In CNC program which letter is used to indicate the sequence number of the block

A] N

B] G

C] F

D] S

180] In CNC program which letter is used to indicate position of linear axis

A] ABC

B] UVW

C] XYZ

D] IJK

181] One of the below letters used in CNC program for Feed rate

A] S

B] F
C] T
D] M
Tool Change & Spindle Speed in CNC Machine.

tool change i cnc.jpg

182] One of the below letters used in CNC program for spindle speed in RPM
A] M
B] T
C] S
D] F
183] In CNC program which letter is used to indicate TOOL function number of tool
A] T
B] S
C] M
D] F
184] In CNC program which miscellaneous function used to program stop
A] M03
B] M00
C] M01
D] M02
CNC Machine Spindle Direction.

cnc machine spindle
direction.png

185] One of the below miscellaneous function used to program optional Stop

A] M 01

B] M 02

C] M 03

D] M 04

186] In CNC program miscellaneous function M02 is used to......

A] Program stop

B] Optional program stop

C] End of program

D] Clockwise spindle on

187] In CNC program miscellaneous function M03 is used to..........

A] Counter clockwise spindle on

B] Clockwise spindle on

C] Spindle off

D] Tool change

Coolant in CNC Machine.

coolant in cnc machine.jpg

188] One of the below miscellaneous function used in CNC program for spindle stop.

A] M04

B] M05

C] M06

D] M07

189] In CNC program which miscellaneous function is used for Tools change

A] M06

B] M07

C] M09

D] M10

190] The size of parts made by .....] for provide interchange ability properties]

(A] Measurement System

(B] Trial and Error System

(C] Limit and Tolerance System

(D] None of Them

191] In Mass Production for Quality Control the Production is Manufacture......

(A] Zero Defects

(B] Try Method]

(C] Trial and Error

(D] In Limit Size

192] Interchange ability is using for.....]

(A] For Maintenance

(B] For Mass Production

(C] For Single Piece Manufacturing

(D] For Trial and Error Method

193] Which one of the following is important factor required to achieve the interchange ability in mass production?]

A] Geometrical accuracy]

B] Standardization

C] Dimensional accuracy

D] Surface finish

194] Interchange ability is normally applied for? _

A] Repairing of parts

B] Mass production

C] Single piece production

D] All of these

195] inspection aims at

A] segregation of defective components

B] conformance of rejection

C] prevention of rejection

D] sale quality goods]

196] Who is responsible for quality?

A] designer

B] inspector

C] operator

D ail]

197] A failure cost reporting system is used for

A] incentive for operators

B] inventory control

C] finding weak points in design

D] finding weak spots in production]

198] The stops and trips are used to

A] minimise delays for measuring and gauging

B] minimise delays in setting tools

C] reduce the number of tools needed

D] reduce the time required to set work]

199] The tern surface finish refers to the...

A] Shining of a machined surface

B] Type of coating given on a surface

C] Heat treatment given on a surface

D] Roughness or smoothness of a surface

200] The purpose for which lapping operation are carried out ---

A] To refine surface finish]

B] To improve quality of fit

C] To improve geometrical accuracy,

D] All the above

201] Which one of the following is a cold working process by which improvement of surface finish, dimensional accuracy and work hardening can be affected without removal of metal?

A] Burnishing

B] Honing

C] Lapping _

D] Super finishing

202] In the honing Process, the movement of the spindle is ---' -----------

A] Vertical and reciprocating

B] Reciprocating

C] Vertical

D] Horizontal and reciprocating

203] lt is the process carried out by using abrasive stick?

A] Lapping

B] Honing

C] Super finishing '

D] Burnishing

204] Which one of the following is important factor required to achieve the interchange ability in mass production?]

A] Geometrical accuracy]

B] Standardization

C] Dimensional accuracy

D] Surface finish

205] Interchange ability is normally applied for? _

A] Repairing of parts

B] Mass production

C] Single piece production

D] All of these

206] Preventive maintenance is ....]

A] The maintenance involves the use of sensitive instruments

B] The maintenance generally performed by operator himself

C] The work carried only when machine break down

D] plan to minimize the unforeseen break down

207] What is a break down maintenance?

A] Maintenance to minimize the unforeseen breakdown

B] Maintenance generally performed by operator himself

C] Maintenance involves replacement of worn out parts

D] Repairs work carried only when machine breakdown

208] The Routine Maintenance is ---------

A] it is planned maintenance to minimize the unforeseen breakdown

B] This type of maintenance involves the use of sensitive instrument

C] It is repair work carried only when machine breakdowns

D] This types of maintenance is generally performed by operator himself

209] The reference surface during marking is provided by the...

A] Surface gauge

B] Workpiece

C] Drawing of the work

D] Marking table surface

210] Lubricant is necessary to ....]

A] run the machine smoothly taking least load

B] Run the machine quickly

C] Stop the machine immediately

D] Produce work piece of greater accuracy

211] Extreme pressure additive (EPA] is mixed with cutting fluid for improving its power of.

A] Cooling

B] Lubrication

D] Production of the machined surface

C] Cleaning of cutting zone

212] The main purpose for using a lubricant in machine tools is to ------

A] Cool down the making parts
B] Prevent machine tool from heating
C] Wet the making parts for close contact
D] Minimize the friction between the making parts
213] Causes the reciprocating movement of connecting rod
A] Connecting rod
B] Lever
C] Cam groove
D] Pawl
214] Lifts the roller at a part of its rotation to actuate the lever
A] Connecting rod
B] Lever
C] Cam groove
D] Pawl
215] instruments rocking movement to the pawl
A] Connecting rod
B] Lever
C] Cam groove
D] Pawl
216] Has rocking movement due to the pivot
A] Connecting rod
B] Lever
C] Cam groove
D] Pawl
217] Drives the ratchet wheel
A] Connecting rod
B] Lever
C] Cam groove
D] Pawl
218] Change In its position varies the feed rate
C] Cam groove
D] Pawl
E] Feed adjust pin
F] Ratchet wheel
219] Rotates the feed shaft]
C] Cam groove
D] Pawl
E] Feed adjust pin

F] Ratchet wheel

220] For transmitting very low torque.

A] Feather key

B] Gib head key

C] Woodruff key

D] Saddle key

221] Profile of key tends to weaken the shaft.

A] Feather key

B] Gib head key

C] Woodruff key

D] Saddle key

222] For transmitting unidirectional torque.

A] Feather key

B] Gib head key

C] Woodruff key

D] Saddle key

223] For transmitting heavy torque.

A] Feather key

B] Gib head key

C] Woodruff key

D] Saddle key

224] For transmitting very high torque of the impact type in both directions of rotation.

A] Gib head key

B] Woodruff key

C] Saddle key

D] Tangential key

225] Permits sliding or axial movement of the mat« ing piece on the shaft.

A] Feather key

B] Gib head key

C] Woodruff key

D] Saddle key

226] Can be withdrawn easily]

A] Feather key

B] Gib head key

C] Woodruff key

D] Saddle key

227] pivoted at the bottom of the base
A] clapper box of shaper
B] rocker arm
C] pawl and ratchet
D] bull gear
228] meant for feed mechanism
A] clapper box of shaper
B] rocker arm
C] pawl and ratchet
D] bull gear
229] helps to tool to lifts up during return stroke
A] clapper box of shaper
B] rocker arm
C] pawl and ratchet
D] bull gear
230] driven by pinion
A] clapper box of shaper
B] rocker arm
C] pawl and ratchet
D] bull gear
231] Can be swivelled while shaping angular surfaces
B] Clapper block
C] Tool post
D] Hinged pen
E] Swivel base
232] it is a device for holding the cutting tool and for setting the depth and position of a cut
A] Clapper box
B] Clapper block
C] Tool post
D] Hinged pen
233] During return stroke the clapper box is free to swivel about it.
A] Clapper box
B] Clapper block
C] Tool post
D] Hinged pen
234] Holds the tool or tool holder rigidly
A] Clapper box

B] Clapper block

C] Tool post

D] Hinged pen

235] Lifts during of return stroke

A] Clapper box

B] Clapper block

C] Tool post

D] Hinged pen

236] The movement of the vertical slide in achieved by stating this part.

D] Hinged pen

E] Swivel base

F] Vertical slide

G] Feed screw handle

237] it carries the saddle

B] rocker arm

C] pawl and ratchet

D] bull gear

E] cross rail

238] it is mounted on bull gear face

A] clapper box of shaper

B] rocker arm

C] pawl and ratchet

D] bull gear

239] it slips during return stroke.

A] clapper box of shaper

B] rocker arm

C] pawl and ratchet

D] bull gear

INDUSTRIAL TRAINING INSTITUTE

Monthly Test-1, Marks- 20, Date:- _______________

(Every Question Carry Two Marks)

1-06] The accuracy of a taper is generally checked by means of......

A] taper gauges

B] gauge blocks

C] indicator and height gauge

2-07] External tapers are checked with

A] limit plug gauge

B] taper ring gauge

C]taper plug gauge

D] thread plug gauge]

3-08] Threading tools are checked for accuracy for the 60? angle by using a

A] Thread plug gauge

B] centre gauge

C] screw pitch gauge

D] tool angle gauge

4-09] The number of threads per inch can be checked with a

A] tool gauge

B] metric rule by counting

C] ring gauge

D] screw pitch gauge

5-10] The accuracy of a taper is generally checked by means of......

A] taper gauges

B] gauge blocks

6-11] External tapers are checked with

A] limit plug gauge

B] taper ring gauge

C]taper plug gauge

D] thread plug gauge]

7-12] Telescopic gauges are used to measure holes and slots]

A] from 10 mm to 100 mm

B] from 12 mm to 152 mm

C] from 12.7 mm to 152.4 mm

D] none of the above]

8-13] Small hole gauges are used to measure holes and slots]

A] below 10 mm

B] below 12.7 mm

C] below 20 mm

D] below 20.7 mm]

9-14] A set of number drill series consists of drills in the following ranges] Indicate the correct range

A] 1 to 40

B] 1 to 50

C] 1 to 80

D] 1 to 100

10-15] The feeler gauge is used for...

A] Checking surface roughness
B] Checking the redius of workpieces
C] Checking the gap between mating parts
D] Checking the accuracy of the hole locators

INDUSTRIAL TRAINING INSTITUTE

Monthly Test-2, Marks- 20, Date:- _______________

(Every Question Carry Two Marks)

1-21] Which one of the following is not an advantage of centre grinding?
A] Easier handling of the woe piece during loading and unloading
B] Handling of the longer work pieces
C] Both shaft and brittle work piece could be handled
D] Low grinding speed

2-22] Straight land surface is cut by tool and cutter grinder with-----------------
A] Plain wheel
B] Cup wheel
C] Conical wheel
D] Disc wheel

3-23] In grinding irregular, curved, tapered, convex and concave surfaces, the grinder used is ~
A] Cylindrical grinder
B] Internal grinder
C] Surface grinder
D] Tool & Cutter grinder]

4-24] Which type of grinding machine Is used for sharpening of tool is milling cutters/drills/hobs/broaches?
A] Chucking]
B] Tool and cutter
C] Centre less
D] Bench

5-25] Which type of grinding wheel is used on tool and cutter grinder to sharpen the milling cutter?
A] Straight cup wheel
B] Flaring cup wheel
C] Dish wheel
D] Saucer wheel

6-26] ....is used on tool and cutter Grinders mainly to sharpen milling cutters and reamers

A] Straight cup

B] Haring cup

C] Dish

D] Recessed both sides

7-27] When using a diamond wheel for cutter grinding, a wheel speed of 1600/mm is recommended] What should be the depth of cut?]

A] 0.005-0.025mm

B] 0.025-0.04mm

C] 0.04-0.05mm

D] 0.05-0.05mm

8-28] Which of the following is precision grinding machine?

A] Pedestal grinding machine

C] Cylindrical surface and Tool & Cutter grinding machine

B] Bench grinding machine

D] Hand grinding machine

9-29] TOOl and cutter are re-shaped by ------------

A] Surface grinding machine

B] tool and cutter grinding machine

C] Cylindrical grinding machine

D] Rotary grinding machine

10-30] Name the part of a tool and cutter grinder on which wheel head is being mounted]

A] Base

B] Saddle

C] Column

D] Table

INDUSTRIAL TRAINING INSTITUTE

Monthly Test-3, Marks- 20, Date:- ______________

(Every Question Carry Two Marks)

1-36] A micrometer has a positive error of 0.02 mm] What is the correct reading when the micrometer measures 25.41 mm?

A] 25.37 mm

B] 25.39 mm

C] 25.43 mm

D] 25.45 mm

2-37] in which one of the following micrometer the graduations on thimble and sleeve are in reverse direction to that of outside micrometer?

A] Inside micrometer

B] Depth micrometer

C] Tube micrometer

D] Flange micrometer

3-38] Micrometer works on the principle of ------

A] Screw

B] Bolt

C] Stud

D] Nut & Screw

4-39] The smallest inside micrometer has the graduation marked on the sleeve

A] 10mm

B] 12mm

C] 13mm

D] 25mm

5-40] The graduations of a depth micrometer is ----------

A] in the reverse direction to that of the outside micrometer both thimble and sleeves

B] In the reverse direction only of the sleeve

C] In the reverse direction only on the thimble

D] Similar to an outside micrometer

6-41] usefulforcutting splines etc.

A] Gear cutting attachment

B] Spherical turning attachment

C] Relieving attachment]

D] None of above

7-42] The angle between the intersecting axes of mating gears.

A] Addendum angle

B] Dedendurn angle

C] Shaft angle

D] Root angle

8-43] The angle between the axis and the root surface of a tooth space.

A] Addendum angle

B] Dedendurn angle

C] Shaft angle

D] Root angle

9-44] The angle between the pitch cone generator and the tip surface of the tooth.

A] Addendum angle

B] Dedendurn angle

C] Shaft angle

D] Root angle

10-45] The angle between the pitch cone generator and the root surface of the tooth.

A] Addendum angle

B] Dedendurn angle

C] Shaft angle

D] Root angle

INDUSTRIAL TRAINING INSTITUTE

Monthly Test-4, Marks- 20, Date:- ______________

(Every Question Carry Two Marks)

1-51]] What is template?

A] One of the cutting operation

B] One of the form turning

C] same figure of the job

D] one of the tool

2-52] Which purpose use template?

A] For marking & checking

B] for threading

C] for turning

D] for measuring

3-53] Which material is use for making template?

A] H.C.S] plate

B] Special tool steel

C] brass or copper

d] G.I] sheet or M.S] thin sheet

4-54] ---------------is used for checking shape of component

A] Template

B] Snap gauge

C] Instrument

D] Sine bar

5-55] For face copying........] Type template is used

A] Rounded

B] Plate type

C] Flat

D] Triangular

6-56] Spindle is perpendicular to the work table

A] Horizontal milling machine
B] Vertical milling machine
C] Universal milling machine]
D] Lathe machine
7-57] The table can be swivelled in horizontal plane
A] Horizontal milling machine
B] Vertical milling machine
C] Universal milling machine]
D] Lathe machine
8-58] The spindle is horizontal to the work table
A] Horizontal milling machine
B] Vertical milling machine
C] Universal milling machine]
D] Lathe machine
9-59] Rigid, sturdy and accommodates heavy work
A] Horizontal milling machine
B] Vertical milling machine
C] Universal milling machine]
D] Lathe machine
10-60] Boring, keyway cutting, profile milling can be done on this machine
A] Horizontal milling machine
B] Vertical milling machine
C] Universal milling machine]
D] Lathe machine

INDUSTRIAL TRAINING INSTITUTE

Monthly Test-5, Marks- 20, Date:- _______________

(Every Question Carry Two Marks)

1-66] This reamer is used where finish is not very critical.
A] Solid fluted machine reamer
B] Chucking reamer
C] Rose reamer
D] Shell reamer
2-67] Several sizes of this reamers are handled with one shank]
A] Solid fluted machine reamer
B] Chucking reamer
C] Rose reamer
D] Shell reamer

3-68] Similar to hand reamer either with straight/left hand helix.

A] Solid fluted machine reamer

B] Chucking reamer

C] Rose reamer

D] Shell reamer

4-69] Similar to jobber reamer but with 'shorter and deeper flutes.

A] Solid fluted machine reamer

B] Chucking reamer

C] Rose reamer

D] Shell reamer

5-70] Other name of this is Jobber reamer]

A] Solid fluted machine reamer

B] Chucking reamer

C] Rose reamer

D] Shell reamer

6-71] This reamer is designed to cut on its end]

A] Solid fluted machine reamer

B] Chucking reamer

C] Rose reamer

D] Shell reamer

7-72] A short reamer with an axial hole used with an arbor or mandrel is called -------

A] Parallel reamer

B] Adjustable reamer

C] Expansion reamer

D] Chucking reamer

8-73] Which one of the following machine reamers is used to correct the misalignment between the reamer axis and the work axis?

A] Floating blade reamer

B] Machine jig reamer]

C] Shell reamer

D] Chucking reamer

9-74] The reamer is used for...

A] Drilling holes in thin sheets

B] Drilling deep holes

C] Removing burrs

D] Enlarging and finishing holes

10-75] The reamer teeth are unevenly spaced because...

A] They are easy to manufacture

B] They can reduce chattering

C] They help to cut metal gradually

D] They help to remove the reamer easily

INDUSTRIAL TRAINING INSTITUTE

Monthly Test-6, Marks- 20, Date:- _______________

(Every Question Carry Two Marks)

1-81] When the taper shank of the drill is larger than the machine spindle, the device to hold the drill is a...

A] Drill sleeve

B] Taper socket

C] Drill drift

D] Chuck and key

2-82] The suitable cutting fluid for drilling mild steel in a drilling machine is...

A] Synthetic soluble oil

B] Neat oil

C] Distilled water

D] Soluble oil

3-83] A special feature of the radial drilling machine is...

A] It can be used for drilling with a H.S.S] drill

B] Table can be moved and set at any position

C] A variety of speeds is available

D] The spindle can be brought to any position

4-84] The point angle of drills depends on...

A] The size of the drill

B] The type of machine

C] The material of the work

D] The RPM of the drill

5-85] The point angle for a standard drill is...

A] 60?

B] 108?

C] 118?

D] 135?

6-86] The helical angle determines the...

A] Cutting angle

B] Chew angle

C] Rake angle

D] Lip angle

7-87] The clearance angle of the drill is between...

A] 3? to 5?

B] 8? to 12?

C] 12? to 20?

D] 15? to 20?

8-88] In a remote place (no electricity available] a rail track is to be drilled] Choose the right drilling machine

A] Radial drilling machine

B] Pillar drilling machine

C] Ratchet drilling machine

D] Sensitive drilling Machine

9- 89] A drilling machine used by a carpenter for cabinet making is a...

A] Ratchet drilling machine

B] Radial drilling machine

C] Breast drilling machine

D] Sensitive drilling machine

10-90] Which one of the following drilling machines is used for drilling holes where electricity is not available?

A] Bench drilling machine

B] Pillar drilling machine

C] Redial drilling machine

D] Ratchet drilling machine

INDUSTRIAL TRAINING INSTITUTE

Monthly Test-7, Marks- 20, Date:- _______________

(Every Question Carry Two Marks)

1-96] How big is the peak amplitude of a sine-wave with an effective value of 220 volts?

A] 311 V

B] 380 V

C] 400 V

D] 440 V

2-97] The peak-to-peak voltage is 99V] how big is the effective value of the sine wave?

A] 70 V

B] 44.5V

C] 49.5 V

D] 35 V

3-98] A moving coil voltmeter reads 10 V AC] How big is the effective voltage?

A] higher

B] lower

C] the same

D] 10% higher

4-99] A moving iron ammeter reads 10 A] how big is the peak current of the oscillation?

A] 7.07 A

B] 1.1414A

C] 70.7 A

D] 14.1 A

5-100] A current of 2 amps flows through a resistance of 10 ohms] The power dissipated in the resistance is equal to...

A] 20 watts

B] 200 watts

C] 40 watts

D] 5 watts

6-101] Power companies are interested in improving the power factor to

A] reduce line current

B] increase motor efficiency

C] increase volt-amperes

D] decrease power

7-102] Moving coil instrument works on the effect of...

A] chemical effect

B] heating effect

C] electrostatic effect

D] electromagnetic effect

8-103] Tape punch having 1 inch in width tape it is made by

A] Paper Mylar

B] Aluminum Mylar

C] Plastic

D] Above all

9-104] In point two point positioning positioning system........] Is acceptable

A] Open loop control system

B] Closed loop control system

C] Above both

D] None of them

10-105] In CNC machine having.......

A] Lead screw

B] Ball lead screw

C] Above both

D] None of both

INDUSTRIAL TRAINING INSTITUTE

Monthly Test-8, Marks- 20, Date:- ______________

(Every Question Carry Two Marks)

1-111] For selection of zero offset before necessary..........

A] cutter is fixed on machine table.

B] The data entered in machine.

C] Job is fixed on machine table.

D] Speed and feed selection necessary before machine operates.

2-112] In zero offset program indicates........] Code of following

A] X y z

B] X0 y0 z00

C] X10 Y20 Z30

D] G71

3-113] Work zero is

A] Datum of machine zero on job position.

B] Indicate by X0Y0Z0.

C] Selection of point on job according to program.

D] The end of machining point

4-114] M command is used for starting operation and complete revolution cycle M03 means.

A] Stop the program.

B] Program completed and reset.

C] Complete the program.

D] Spindle clockwise motion.

5-115] CNC machine is not manually operated it is control by...........

A] Program

B] operation

C] Cam

D] Plug board system

6-116] In CNC machine M13 means

A] coolant stop

B] coolant on

C] spindle stop

D] coolant on & spindle on

7-117] The function of power pack in CNC machine.

A] For balancing of lubricants heat.

B] For increasing heat of lubricants.

C] For destroy heat of lubricant.

D] Above all.

8-118] The section of CNC machine bed is.....

A] Flat

B] Half round

C] Rectangular

D] Triangular

9-119] Following which statement is disadvantage of CNC machine.

A] Less inspection charge.

B] Less tooling charge.

C] Increase production rate.

D] High establishment charge.

10-120] The point to point system is more effective for......

A] Turning

B] Profile milling

C] Grinding

D] Drilling

INDUSTRIAL TRAINING INSTITUTE

Monthly Test-9, Marks- 20, Date:- _______________

(Every Question Carry Two Marks)

1-126] One of the below miscellaneous function used in CNC program for coolant on

A] M08

B] M09

C] M10

D] M11

2-127] One of the below miscellaneous function in CNC program used for coolant off

A] M11

B] M10

C] M9

D] M15

3-128] In CNC program which miscellaneous function used for clamping the job on machine table.

A] M09

B] M10

C] M11

D] M15

4-129] One of the below miscellaneous function in CNC program used for unclamp the job

A] M11

B] M15

C] M30

D] M60

5-130] In CNC program which miscellaneous function used for change of workpiece

A] M30

B] M60

C] M68

D] M78

6-131] The machine is.........for zero off-setting on CNC Machine.

A] In MDI Mode

B] In JOG Mode

C] In Automatic Mode

D] In Present Mode

7-132] The feed rate on NC Machine is indicate by ......code.

A] X

B] Y

C] F

D] Z

8-133] The position of axis is indicate by.......code.

A] X,Y,Z

B] P,Q,R

C] A,B,C

D] M,N,O

9-134] CNC Drilling Machine is on.......Axis Programmed.

A] Two Axis

B] Three Axis

C] Four Axis

D] Six Axis

10-135] From.......unit collect instruction in control unit of CNC

A] Machine Tool

B] Instruction

C] Magnetic Box

D] Memory

INDUSTRIAL TRAINING INSTITUTE

Monthly Test-10, Marks- 20, Date:- _______________

(Every Question Carry Two Marks)

1-141] CNC Machine means.......

A] Natural Control Machine

B] Pneumatic control Machine

C] Numerical Control Machine

D] No Command Machine

2-142] Following which advantage of Pneumatic power system

A] For increase production rate.

B] Less cash for layout

C] Good climate for work

D] Above all

3-143] For face copying........] Type template is used

A] Rounded

B] Plate type

C] Flat

D] Triangular

4-144].............. Is Main principle of CNC MACHINE?

A] Indicate all states in numbers

B] More time required for mechanical control on machine.

C] Cutting speed is more than manual control.

D] Production sequence in workshop is stored by block number in machine.

5-145] For copy of one shaft............Type template is used.

A] Rounded

B] Triangular

C] Flats

D] Square

6-146] The symptoms of continuous path is

A] Called counting system.

B] Tool and work piece on co-ordinate Axis for inter related motion.

C] By the setting of cutter feed and speed

D] Above all

7-147] Misc command M30 means........

A] End of program and reset

B] Program stop

C] Clockwise motion of spindle

D] Complete the programs

8-148] Following which affect on milling surface while by milling with unsetting spindle vertical milling machine with- longitudinal feed.

A] Convex surface

B] Concave surface

C] Radius cross line

D] Rough surface

9-149] While milling by vertical milling machine with 12 mm dia end mill cutter through slot provide on mild steel plate the cutter is sleep and broken for this fault how it is avoid.

A] High speed spindle

B] Low cutting speed

C] Increase of cut depth

D] Less the depth and feed of cutter

10-150] Having 5 mm pitch of screw and dividing ratio of 40 : 1 what is lead of milling machine

A] 0.25 mm

B] 5 mm

C] 8 mm

D] 200 mm

INDUSTRIAL TRAINING INSTITUTE

Monthly Test-11, Marks- 20, Date:- ______________

(Every Question Carry Two Marks)

1-151] If not use of backlash Eliminator slap cutter used for down milling operation which safety to be observed?

A] Less lead and depth

B] High lead

C] high lead and less depth

D] High lead and high speed

2-152] Zero offset is the distance between.....] And.........

A] G41 & g42

B] Machine zero & work zero

C] Reference point and tapping mode

D] None of them

3-153] The feed rate is programmed as mm per minute with G ....] And mm per- Revolution with G.

A] G41 & g42

B] G 43 and G 40

C] G 94 and g95

D] None of them

4-154] For collection all instructions from.......] In CNC control unit

A] Memory

B] Tape reader

C] Control panel

D] Operator

5-155] For control forward and backward of- CNC drilling machine y axis.........

A] Spindle

B] Table

C] Clockwise

D] Column

6-156] M 01 command means.....

A] For stopping programs

B] End of program and reset

C] Stopping programs condition

D] Clockwise rotation of machine spindle

7-157] CNC machine is founded by American scientist john person in.......] Year

A] 1950

B] 1952

C] 1955

D] 1957

8-158] Name of unit used to command the CNC machine.

A] Control unit

B] Memory unit

C] Input unit

D] Output unit

9-159] Name of unit used to processing the data in CNC machine.

A] Memory unit

B] Control unit

C] Input unit

D] Output unit

10-160] Name of unit used to storing the data in CNC machine.

A] Input unit

B] Control unit

C] Memory unit

D] Output unit

INDUSTRIAL TRAINING INSTITUTE

Monthly Test-12, Marks- 20, Date:- ______________

(Every Question Carry Two Marks)

1-161] Name of unit used to calculation of data in CNC machine.

A] Output unit

B] Arithmetic unit

C] Memory unit

D] Input unit

2-162] Name of unit used to display result of processing data in CNC machine

A] Arithmetic unit

B] Output unit

C] Memory unit

D] Input unit

3-163] Servo Motor in CNC machine is used to.............

A] Changing tool on machine spindle

B] Driving machine spindle

C] Fixing job on machine spindle

D] Proving job on spindle

4-164] One of the below part of CNC machine used to changing tools on spindle.

A] Servo Motor

B] Control panel

C] Automatic tool changer A T C

D] High speed spindle

5-165] One of the below CNC machine in CNC milling category is.......

A] Chucking centre

B] CNC late

C] Vertical machining centre

6-171] One of the bellow preparatory function G 00 is used in CNC program for.........

A] Linear interpellation or feed motion in straight line.

B] Clockwise circular interpellation

C] Point to point Positioning or Rapid motion.

D] Counter clockwise circular interpellation

7-172] One of the bellow preparatory function used in CNC program for 3D interpellation

A] G 05

B] G12

C] G17

D] G18

8-173] One of the bellow preparatory you function used in CNC program for thread cutting constant lead

A] G33

B] G40

C] G53

D] G62

9-174] One of the bellow preparatory function used in CNC program for tapping operation.

A] G-40

B] G53

C] G62

D] G63

10-175] One of the below preparatory function used in CNC program for milling operation.

A] G62

B] G63

C] G 78, 79

D] G81

www.ingramcontent.com/pod-product-compliance
Ingram Content Group UK Ltd.
Pitfield, Milton Keynes, MK11 3LW, UK
UKHW021921190726
13853UKWH00002B/772

9 798888 696941